THE I T
RENAISSANC

James Hankins, (

HUMANIST EDUCATIONAL
TREATISES

HUMANIST EDUCATIONAL TREATISES

TRANSLATED BY

CRAIG W. KALLENDORF

THE I TATTI RENAISSANCE LIBRARY
HARVARD UNIVERSITY PRESS
CAMBRIDGE, MASSACHUSETTS
LONDON, ENGLAND
2008

Series design by Dean Bornstein

Library of Congress Cataloging-in-Publication Data

Humanist educational treatises / translated by Craig W. Kallendorf.
p.   cm. — (The I Tatti Renaissance library)
Text in English only.
Includes bibliographical references and index.
ISBN-13: 978-0-674-03087-9 (pbk. : alk. paper)
1. Education, Humanistic — Italy.
2. Education — Italy — History — To 1500 — Sources.
3. Renaissance — Italy.   I. Kallendorf, Craig.
LA108H867 2008
370.11′20945 — dc22   2008016232

Contents

ॐॐॐ

Introduction   vii

PIER PAOLO VERGERIO
The Character and Studies Befitting a Free-Born Youth   1

LEONARDO BRUNI
The Study of Literature   47

AENEAS SILVIUS PICCOLOMINI
The Education of Boys   65

BATTISTA GUARINO
A Program of Teaching and Learning   133

Note on the Translations   161

Notes   163

Bibliography   187

Index   189

Introduction

❧✦❧

The cycle of disciplines we call the humanities emerged in their modern form during the Italian Renaissance, around the turn of the fifteenth century. The humanities (or *studia humanitatis*) came into existence as the result of an educational and cultural reform movement led by scholars, teachers, writers, and civic leaders who are today known as humanists. The humanist movement, as defined by most modern scholars, developed in Italy during the fourteenth century out of the medieval rhetorical tradition in response to the challenge of scholastic education. The overwhelming emphasis of medieval scholastic education was on practical, pre-professional, and scientific studies; it prepared men to be doctors, lawyers, or professional theologians and taught primarily from approved textbooks in logic, natural philosophy, medicine, law, and theology. Humanist educators reacted against this utilitarian approach to education. They believed education should have a moral purpose and should fit youths to take up leadership roles in courts and civic life. The best way to bring about this result, they believed, was to immerse young men and women in the best literature of classical antiquity, especially its poetry, history, oratory, and moral philosophy. Renaissance humanists, in contrast with medieval university professors, aimed to educate an entire social and political elite, male and female alike, and not just the male, pre-professional portion of it. In language borrowed from classical antiquity, they claimed to teach "free men," people who did not have to work for a living—hence the expression *artes liberales*. Humanist educators aimed to create a particular type of person: men and women who would be virtuous because they had read and identified with powerful examples of classical virtue; who would be prudent because they had extended their human experience into the

distant past through the study of history; and who would be eloquent, able to communicate virtue and prudence to others, because they had studied the most eloquent writers and speakers of
the past.

The early humanists were thus reformers of a special kind: not
the kind who want to reform institutions, but the kind who want
to leave institutions mostly intact while improving the quality of
the human material that directs those institutions. It could be said
that they were Aristotelian, not Platonic reformers; they aimed to
achieve the good of communities through "social customs and
mental culture,"[1] not social and political engineering. The great
tool for this transformation of mankind was classical education:
the canonical works of classical literature, which because they had
such desirable effects were called *bonae litterae* ("good letters") or
litterae humaniores ("more humane letters"). They were letters that
made you morally better and more civilized. People who taught
litterae humaniores in Italian schools and universities began to be
called *humanistae* toward the end of the fifteenth century, and that
was the semantic root upon which the later term "humanism" was
built. Humanistic education of this type became immensely popular in Italy in the half century between 1390 and 1440 and spread
to Northern Europe at the end of the fifteenth century; it remained entrenched in European educational systems down to the
twentieth century.

The four treatises in this volume, along with Maffeo Vegio's *On
Education and Excellence of Character in Children*,[2] represent the full-
est expression of the Italian humanists' theory of education. As
actually practiced by famous schoolmasters such as Gasparino
Barzizza (1360–1430) at Padua and Pavia, Vittorino da Feltre
(1370–1446) at Mantua, and Guarino da Verona (1374–1460) at
Ferrara, humanist education gradually enlarged the number of

Latin authors included in the curriculum and added the study of Greek language and literature; it worked to help students distinguish the values and manner of expression of antiquity from those inherited from medieval Christendom. Although it generally remained compatible with the prevailing Christian values of its day, humanist education, as it spread through the schools and universities of Italy and Europe, facilitated the separation of a classical vision of humanity from its medieval Christian coloring, leading in later generations to the basically secular school curricula that prevailed through the beginning of the last century.

The treatises of Vergerio, Bruni, Piccolomini, and Guarino are not the only expressions of humanist educational theory, but they are the most influential. In the English-speaking world, William H. Woodward directed attention to them more than a century ago, but their popularity goes back to the Renaissance itself.[3] These treatises, along with two important works of ancient pedagogy, St. Basil's *Letter to Young Men* (translated by Leonardo Bruni) and pseudo-Plutarch's essay *On the Education of Children* (translated by Guarino da Verona), formed the nucleus of Italian humanist pedagogical writings and were all printed numerous times in the fifteenth and sixteenth centuries. Even before the invention of printing, when books were still prepared laboriously by hand, the material presented here was copied over and over again: Leonardo Bruni's treatise, for example, was copied at least 127 times and printed 15 times,[4] and Pier Paolo Vergerio's treatise survives in more than 300 manuscripts and 40 printed editions.

Born in Capodistria on (perhaps) July 23, 1370, Pier Paolo Vergerio studied and taught the arts, medicine, and law in Padua, Florence, and Bologna, combining a teaching career with service to the church and to the Holy Roman Emperor Sigismund. His writings reflect this broad range of interests, running from a treatise on metrics (*De arte metrica*) and a comedy (*Paulus*) in the tradition of the Roman dramatist Terence, to works on St. Jerome and on the schism within the church. He died in Budapest on July 8, 1444.

The Character and Studies Befitting a Free-Born Youth, which was written ca. 1402–1403, has several features in common with the other treatises in this volume. For one thing, it has a pronounced moralizing flavor: education must make the student virtuous as well as learned, and even games should be chosen with an eye to the improvement of character. Second, the program outlined here is designed to produce not scholars but educated princes and aristocrats, men of affairs whose lives are guided and enriched by books but not limited to them alone. Virtue and glory are the ends of education, and the disciplines to be studied are those appropriate to a free man who, like his ancestors in Greece and Rome, moves easily between arms and letters. Yet among these common chords, some distinctive strains sound in Vergerio's treatise. He goes back to the Greeks, for example, for an approach to education that is based on a fourfold division amongst letters, gymnastics, music, and drawing, and he develops at unusual length the idea that everyone has different talents and that any general program must be adapted to the strengths and weaknesses of each student.

Leonardo Bruni (1370–1444) was the son of a grain merchant in Arezzo, a city near Florence. Bruni began the study of law at the University of Florence in the 1390s but soon fell under the influence of Coluccio Salutati, the most important disciple of Francesco Petrarca. In 1397–99 he studied Greek under the Byzantine émigré Manuel Chrysoloras, and so became one of the first Westerners of the Renaissance to learn that tongue. He served as apostolic secretary under four popes (Innocent VII, Gregory XII, Alexander V, and John XXIII), then returned to Florence, where he worked independently as a scholar. In 1427 he was was chosen to be Florence's chancellor (or secretary of state) and served in that post until his death.

Bruni was the best-selling literary author of the fifteenth century, the leading scholar of his generation, and deeply involved in the effort to stimulate greater interest in and emulation of Italy's classical past. Much (perhaps too much) scholarly attention of late has been devoted to Bruni's "civic humanism," in which he participated in a broader effort to make classical scholarship serve the political needs of his day, but his achievements are much greater than this might suggest. For one thing, he replaced the medieval word-for-word translation with a new style of translation according to sense, a technique he used to make many important Greek texts, including works of Plato, Aristotle, Plutarch, and Demosthenes, available to the educated readers of his time. He developed new standards for evaluating historical evidence, which led to an important work, his *History of the Florentine People*.[5] And his *laudatio* of the city of Florence and the dialogue he addressed to his friend Vergerio revived classical forms by infusing them with content of contemporary interest.

The treatise *The Study of Literature* (written between 1422 and 1429, perhaps in 1424) holds a modest but significant place within Bruni's prolific scholarly output. It does not set out a full educational program, but focuses on which authors to read and how to read them. It emphasizes rhetoric rather less than the other treatises in its genre, and religious authors rather more, which probably results from its being addressed, unlike the other works in this volume, to a woman. Its brevity, however, perhaps allows a key principle to come through with unusual clarity: the idea that the ancients should be studied not as an antiquarian exercise but as the source for wisdom to live by and for a linguistic facility that fosters clear thinking and persuasive communication.

Aeneas Sylvius Piccolomini was born on October 18, 1405, the eldest of eighteen children in a family of exiled Sienese nobility. He received a good education, first from a parish priest in his native town of Corsignano, then at the University of Siena, after which he made his way to the Council of Basel, where he found employment among a succession of those who wanted to subordinate the authority of the Pope to that of the Council. This experience led to one of his major literary works, the *Commentary on the Council of Basel*, and his election as secretary to the antipope Felix v. He then found employment in the curia of the Emperor Frederick III, for whom he performed a variety of services. He was ordained a priest in 1446 and made his peace with the papacy, becoming Cardinal of Siena, then Pope himself, assuming the name of Pius II. During his six-year papacy, he worked tirelessly to stimulate a crusade to regain control of Constantinople from the Turks, a project which died with him on August 14, 1464.

The Education of Boys (1450) takes its place among some two dozen works of Piccolomini's, most of them historical and literary in nature. It was written for Ladislaus, king of Austria, Bohemia, and Hungary, and is divided into two main parts, dealing respectively with the training of the body and that of the mind. The first, shorter part considers physical education and self-control, with moderation in all things being the guide. In training the mind, religious education is treated first, followed by a detailed program of reading and study. Learning rests on grammar, divided into its traditional parts: speaking correctly, reading model authors, and writing. Like other humanists of his day, Piccolomini focuses his remarks regarding model authors on rhetoricians, historians, poets, and moral philosophers; any writers that might threaten the student's character or faith are to be either excluded entirely or read in expurgated editions. He then turns to the other liberal arts and recommends that the young king should have some knowledge, but not too much, of rhetoric, logic, arithmetic, geometry, music, and astronomy.

Battista Guarino was born in 1434, the youngest son of the great humanist teacher Guarino da Verona. He was educated by his father in the methods developed at Ferrara, where Guarino served as tutor to the ruling Este family and maintained his celebrated school. The elder Guarino's school was the most famous in Europe and attracted young men from as far as Scandinavia and England. At the age of twenty-one Battista Guarino took up the chair of rhetoric in Bologna, but two years later he returned to Ferrara. Here he wrote his educational treatise, which serves as a general record of practices in Guarino's school. On his father's death, Battista took over his professorship at the university, where he specialized in textual emendation and worked extensively on the manuscripts of the Roman poet Catullus.

A Program of Teaching and Learning (1459) provides a detailed introduction to the elementary level of instruction that Bruni, for example, preferred to pass over, and its focus on orderly method reflects clearly the practice of a teacher. The subject of the treatise is grammar, which is divided into two parts: the first is called "methodical" (that is, *methodos*), which lays out the paradigms of all the parts of speech; the other is called "historical," which gives a detailed treatment of historical knowledge and past achievements (cap. 8). The discussion of "method" includes representative observations on the forms of Latin words and on meter, while the "historical" section unfolds into a survey of the canon of humanist authors, with a much greater emphasis on Greek than in, for example, Piccolomini's work.

These treatises offer significant rewards to the modern reader, but they must be approached on their own terms, not ours. Anyone who comes to these texts with post-romantic notions of originality, for example, is likely to be disappointed. All four of these authors wrote with an eye on those who went before them, and their contemporaries measured their achievement in relation to how well they knew their predecessors and how successfully they integrated their sources into a new work that met the needs of their day without losing the aura of antiquity. Fifteenth-century educators had a technique for accomplishing this: the commonplace book, in which students created headings that might be useful to them in the future, then collected precepts and stories from their reading that illustrated that heading. The four treatises on educational theory in this volume were clearly composed according to this technique, which requires a modern editor to retrace the background studies of these authors through a collection of sources that may surprise the modern reader who is unfamiliar with past practices of reading and writing.

The writers of these treatises found material in a number of ancient sources. Quintilian's *Education of the Orator* was particularly important, since it outlined in great detail the pedagogical theory and practice of ancient Rome. The treatise *On the Education of Children* (attributed to Plutarch during the Renaissance) and St. Basil's *Letter to Young Men on Reading Pagan Literature* were both echoed again and again in these four works. As sources for precepts and shorter stories, we find regular reliance on Greek and Latin authors that are still well known today, like Cicero, Seneca, and Plutarch, along with those that were far more popular in the fifteenth century than in the twenty-first, like Aulus Gellius, Vegetius, and Valerius Maximus. And there are occasional sources that seem to have been more important to one of these educational theorists than to the others: Piccolomini, for example, follows Quintilian closely and shows a surprising fondness for John of Salisbury, Bruni's treatise reveals his deep study of Cicero, while Vergerio's treatise has a pronounced Aristotelian flavor.

From the vantage point of the twenty-first century, one might also wonder how well the lofty precepts of these treatises actually shaped what went on the early modern classroom. Classroom practice, as opposed to theory, is best illuminated by the collections of lecture notes that fill European libraries, and while much work still needs to be done on these notes, preliminary analysis suggests that in the hands of an uninspired teacher, daily work tended to resemble Piccolomini's spelling rules more than Vergerio's musings on the ennobling effects of reading and study.[6]

We should not, however, overemphasize this point. The documents of the period also attest how inspiring teachers like Vittorino da Feltre and Guarino da Verona were, and what they did in the classroom is reflected in the four treatises presented here. In a surprisingly short time, these principles changed the shape of European education and, in one form or another, could still be recognized in the French *lycée*, the Italian *liceo classico*, or the German *Gymnasium* of the twentieth century. As we enter the twenty-first century, it will be interesting to see how current trends in education develop, but it is difficult to imagine that these four treatises will entirely lose their relevance for teachers and students who care about accurate expression, moral character, and a sense of connection to the past of our civilization.

I wish to express my appreciation to my colleague Christoph Konrad, who read through a draft of my translations of Vergerio and Battista Guarino and suggested a good many improvements. Leah Whittington made numerous useful suggestions. I would also like to thank the series editor, James Hankins, whose work on this volume went far beyond the usual editorial labors. This volume is dedicated to my son Trevor, in the hope that he, too, might profit from the wisdom it contains.

Craig W. Kallendorf
July 2001

NOTES

1. Aristotle, *Pol.* II.5, 1263b.

2. To be translated in a future volume of *ITRL* edited by Craig Kallendorf and Christoph Konrad.

3. William H. Woodward, *Studies in Education during the Age of the Renaissance 1450–1600* (Cambridge: Cambridge University Press, 1906; reprint New York: Columbia University Press, 1967).

4. See James Hankins, *Repertorium Brunianum: A Critical Guide to the Writings of Leonardo Bruni*, vol. 1 (Rome: Istituto storico italiano per il Medio Evo, 1997), *ad indices*.

5. Books I–IV have appeared in this series: Leonardo Bruni, *History of the Florentine People*, *vol. 1: Books I–IV*, edited and translated by James Hankins, I Tatti Renaissance Library, vol. 3 (Cambridge, Mass.: Harvard University Press, 2001).

6. See Anthony Grafton and Lisa Jardine, *From Humanism to the Humanities: Education and the Liberal Arts in Fifteenth- and Sixteenth-Century Europe* (Cambridge, Mass.: Harvard University Press, 1986).

HUMANIST EDUCATIONAL
TREATISES

PIER PAOLO VERGERIO
THE CHARACTER AND STUDIES
BEFITTING A FREE-BORN YOUTH
DEDICATED TO
UBERTINO DA CARRARA

Preface

We understand, Ubertino, that Francesco the elder, your grand-   1
father[1] — whose many magnificent deeds are on record just as his
many wise sayings are remembered everywhere — used to say there
were three ways that parents could easily serve the interests of
their children, and were with good reason obliged to do so. One
was to call them by honorable names. For to have been allotted an
unseemly name is no small deprivation, as it might be in a matter
of little importance. This mistake is generally made by a few people who irresponsibly want credit for making up new names or
who pass down trustingly to their posterity as a family inheritance
any names they have received from their ancestors. Second, parents should settle their children in renowned cities. For the pres-
tige and distinction of one's country matters a great deal, both in
regard to wealth and glory, and in regard to what Francesco put in
third place and we shall shortly describe. To be sure, the situation
often arises that is exemplified by the Athenian Themistocles' response in debate to a certain native of Seriphos, who was arguing
that Themistocles owed his fame, not to his own virtue, but to his
fatherland. Themistocles said, "You would not be famous even if
you were an Athenian, nor would I be undistinguished if I were a
Seriphian."[2] The third point was that parents should instruct their
children in the liberal arts.

2   All of these points are excellent ones, as might be expected coming from a man who was considered — and who was — the wisest man of his time in general knowledge, but the last point above all is especially profitable. For parents can provide their children with no more lasting resources, no more dependable protection in life than instruction in honorable arts and liberal disciplines. With such an endowment, children can usually overcome and bring distinction to obscure family origins and humble homelands. For anyone is legally permitted to change his name, provided it is done without deception, and no one is forbidden to change his residence whenever he pleases. But if someone is not educated from youth in the liberal arts, or if he is infected with illiberal training, there is little hope that in later years, of his own accord, he can just cast aside the latter or take up the former without difficulty. In youth, therefore, the foundations for living well are to be laid, and the mind must be trained to virtue while it is young and impressionable, for the mind will preserve throughout life the impressions it takes on now.[3] But although it is fitting that everyone (and parents especially) desire to educate their children correctly, and that children be such that they may seem worthy of good parents,[4] it is particularly fitting that those of lofty rank, who cannot say or do anything in secret,[5] be instructed in the principal arts in such a way as to be held worthy of the fortune and rank they possess. For it is only fair that those who wish all the greatest things to be due themselves, be themselves obliged to excel in the greatest things. Nor is there any more firm or solid rationale for ruling than this: that those who rule be judged by all to be the worthiest to rule.

3   So I am delighted, Ubertino, first, that you have been given a name which has long been renowned in your family and recently made glorious by the one who was the sixth, counting backwards, of your family to have held power;[6] second, that you were born in

this most ancient and royal city, which flourishes in the study of all the liberal arts and abounds in all the things that people use, the descendant of a family of princes and of a father who is himself a prince, under whose leadership the happy state of the city and the renown of your family name increases daily. And finally, I am delighted, both for the sake of my faith in you and the benevolence you and your family have shown me, to see you inclined, thanks to your father's diligence and especially to your own judgment, to devote great effort to the liberal arts and the most excellent intellectual activities. For even if the three things we have mentioned look like the things we most desire from our parents (and I am certainly not going to deny that each of them is extremely important), it is still parents who name their children, and chance, not choice, that gives a man his country. But everyone acquires for himself the liberal arts and virtue itself, and these are the most desirable things a person can seek. For wealth, glory, pleasures—these are transitory and fleeting. Character, however, and the fruits of the virtues endure undiminished and last forever.[7]

So if I advise you to be diligent in your studies, I nevertheless   4 observe that this advice, however willingly offered, is quite unnecessary. For what else can I advise you to do, than what you are always doing? What person can I recommend to you as a model of virtue other than yourself? Since you have evidently been endowed by nature herself with gifts of mind and body, so that one might legitimately hope for all great things from you, and since you also excel in all important activities, so that you surpass not only the hope but even the prayers of all, how could anyone's exhortations or example possibly motivate you more strongly?[8] Hence it is in your name that I have undertaken this little work, and have begun writing to you about the character and studies befitting a free-born youth—that is, what is fitting for young gentlemen to practice and what they should avoid—not, indeed, to advise you, but to advise others of this age through you. And when I lay out what others should do, you will recognize in yourself what you yourself are already doing.

5 Because a person is composed of soul and body, those to whom strength of body and intellect has been given seem to me to have gained something great from nature. For since we see very many people who through no fault of their own were born slow of mind and weak in body, how much should we thank nature if we are strong and whole in both! The thanks that are due to nature, moreover, will be paid if we have not neglected her gifts but rather taken care to cultivate them through the right sort of studies in the liberal arts. First, therefore, everyone of his own accord should look to his own abilities; or, if we are not yet of responsible years, our parents and the others who care for us should attend to this; and it will be fitting that we turn our attention particularly to those studies for which we are naturally inclined and suited, and to devote ourselves entirely to them.[9] But those especially to whom nature has given an intellect worthy of free men should not be allowed to languish in sloth nor be caught up in illiberal affairs.

The Signs of a Liberal Temper

6 Generally speaking, the first mark of a liberal temper is that it is motivated by eagerness for praise and inflamed by love of glory;[10] this is the source of a certain noble envy and a striving without hatred for praise and excellence. The next sign is that it willingly obeys its elders and is not defiant toward those who give good advice. For as horses are considered better for fighting when they are easily controlled by hand and rear up with their ears perked at the

blare of trumpets, so those youths who listen well to their mentors and whom praise motivates to do what is good seem to offer hope of rich fruit.[11] For since they lack experience of life and are unable to grasp rationally the true good of virtue and the face of moral rectitude[12] — which, if it were visible to the eyes, would of itself arouse a wondrous longing for wisdom, as Plato says and Cicero recalls[13] — the next best motive, after this [highest] one, is the desire to aim at the best out of eagerness for glory and praise.

Furthermore, those who are keen for endeavor, flee inaction, and always love to do what is right seem well disposed by nature, for (to employ the same sort of simile) as horses are considered better runners when they leap forward straightaway once the signal has been given and do not stand sluggishly in place awaiting the spur or the whip, so young men who, without someone to admonish them, return eagerly at the appointed hours to their customary studies and to exercises that have scarcely been interrupted should be considered outstandingly suited to works of virtue. But even if they fear threats and blows, how much better it is when they fear dishonor and disgrace, for from these is born shame, the best indicator of virtue at that age. So it is good if they blush when scolded and become better and love their teachers after chastisement, for this, too, is a sign that they love discipline.[14]

Indeed, we must have no less hope that those who are by nature kind and easily placated will achieve moral excellence. For minds and bodies are similar in this respect: as in the case of the latter it is the sign of a good constitution that the stomach does not reject food, but digests everything easily and turns it into nourishment for the body's members, so it is the sign of a naturally well-constituted mind that it does not hate or scorn anyone but puts the best construction on whatever is said or done. Much evidence about behavior can be derived in this way, but as far as the condition of the body is concerned, soft bodies make ready minds, as Aristotle has written.[15] For the rest, one should consult those who claim that everyone's intellect and native character can be apprehended through physiognomy, an entire line of reasoning which we may [here] leave aside.

9   Generally, however, one can perceive from our innate qualities in youth, as we have said, what sort of men we are going to be. For from their earliest years nature brings forth in certain people signs of future virtue, like little flowers. Hence we call gifted those young men who seem to promise well of themselves on the basis of their facial expression, their bearing, and their other actions. As it is base for young men such as these to deceive expectation, so praise is given to those who without any such indication have nevertheless turned out well, having imitated a certain kind of apple which under an ugly and rough skin preserves a sweet flavor. In this connection Socrates used to give good advice, that young men should often look at their own image in a mirror. His reasoning evidently was that those who had a fine appearance would not dishonor it with vices, while those whose appearance was more irregular would take care to make themselves attractive through their virtues.[16]

10   But perhaps they will have better success if they will contemplate, not their own image, but the behavior of someone else of high character, a living mirror. For if Publius Scipio and Quintus Fabius used to say that they were deeply inspired by gazing upon the images of famous men[17] — an experience common to nearly all noble minds — if Julius Caesar was spurred on to supreme power after seeing the image of Alexander the Great,[18] what, in all reason, is bound to occur when someone can gaze on a living effigy and an example [of virtue] that is still breathing? True, the images of our ancestors perhaps inspire us to rival them in glory still more, since the actual presence of a person generally diminishes his glory and the living are usually beset with envy. But this at any rate is certain, that the living character of a man, like his living

voice, is more powerful as an example of virtue and character as well as for teaching of any kind.[19] Thus a young man inclined toward study who is aroused by the desire for virtue and true glory ought to select one man or a number of men who seem morally excellent to him, and whose life and character he will imitate to the extent that his age will allow. Those men and older men in general should maintain at all times a consistent pattern of gravity and discretion, but especially in the presence of their juniors,[20] for the young are inclined to make mistakes, and unless they are restrained by the example and authority of their elders, they will always slip easily into worse conduct.

The Character of Youth

And since their behavior is suited to their age (which is true of other ages as well), those who are good should be strengthened and assisted through practice and precept, but those who are bad and blameworthy should be corrected. Of this latter group, some are only following their nature; others lack experience; while others suffer both deficiencies.[21] [The young] are especially generous and liberal by nature because they have not experienced need[22] and have not sought wealth for themselves by their own effort; it is unusual for one who has amassed wealth by his own efforts to waste it rashly. At the same time, because their heat and blood overflow into the growth as well as the nourishment of their bodies, whereas the opposite happens in old men for the opposite reason, what sort of old man can we hope for him to be, if he is [already] grasping and greedy in his youth?[23] This is not to say that they should be allowed to distribute largess; they do not [yet] know how to discriminate properly among gifts, persons, and merit.[24] But [avarice] is the sign of a corrupt nature and an illiberal temper.[25]

11

12   Such students, then, perform manual labor so as to make money in trade, or they engage in business to take care of their families, especially those who, even if they were of a nobler sort and at some time or other pursued the arts, nevertheless always reduce them, like everything else, to ignoble gain — something indeed which is thoroughly foreign to noble minds. Then there are those with high hopes who readily promise themselves many great things, above all a long life, like those in whom natural heat abounds, as though that were sufficient for every time and every task. And on this account they are magnanimous and high-spirited, because it is a property of heat to carry things upwards.[26] Hence they become arrogant and, as Horace puts it,

> harsh to those who try to advise them[27]

and rude to others, while exalting themselves. They want to excel and, for this reason, because they want to be seen as in the know, they are quick to reveal secrets and are generally discovered to be liars when boasting about themselves.[28] And because they are in-experienced at the same time, they think they tell the truth but are deceived in many things.[29]

13   They should be discouraged most of all from the vanity of ly-ing, first because, after they have become used to it in youth, they preserve this, the worst of all habits, in their mature years;[30] then because almost nothing offends their elders more than the lying of young men who, though born yesterday, try to get around old men with their deceptions. It helps, too, if the young are warned to say little and to speak seldom, unless bidden to do so. For in much talk there is always something that can be criticized. But if one must err in either direction, it is certainly much safer to be silent than to speak. If one is silent at the wrong time, one errs only in being silent, but in speaking at the wrong time, one may err in many things.[31] We should also take care that the young do not be-

come accustomed to base and dishonorable speech, for as a Greek poet has said, and the apostle Paul has repeated,

bad conversation corrupts good character.[32]

Moreover, in accordance with our earlier line of reasoning, in- 14
sofar as the young are eager for excellence, they are also modest,[33] since they are afraid to be shamed and remember the recent re-buke of their parents and teacher, and since at the same time they are also inexperienced, they think they can be easily refuted. Again, they are excessively credulous, for lacking worldly experi-ence, they believe that whatever they hear is true.[34] Also, their opinions change easily, since their humors are in motion due to growth and they have in abundance the heat which is the principle cause of motion. The soul, in fact, follows the complexion of the body, and thus, just as those who lack something are quick to de-sire it, so they are swiftly satisfied once they have obtained what they want. The young follow their passions above all and do every-thing with great vigor because they have keen desires which their bodily heat spurs on, while the rational powers and prudence that could moderate their desires are weak.[35] But, as Terence's Sosias says: for my part

I think that the most useful thing in life is
that all things happen agreeably and nothing to excess.[36]

They are also compassionate and uncorrupt, since they were born not long before and have uncorrupt blood, and they judge others according to their own relative innocence, and so believe them to suffer unjustly.[37] But they take the greatest pleasure in their friendships and love the clubs they belong to,[38] which they gener-ally join and abandon on the same day.

Instruction, then, should be given in conformity with these 15
considerations, and good behavior must be acquired and bad be-

havior either curtailed or entirely rooted out. And indeed, as regards the guardianship of youth, although much is permitted to domestic discipline, some things are nevertheless customarily delimited by law—I might almost have said that everything should be.[39] For it is in the public interest that the young people in our cities be well-behaved, and if our youth are brought up properly, this will be useful indeed to our cities and good for them as well. But to speak more specifically, they are to be kept most of all from those sins into which they are easily and naturally led by their age. For every age has certain vices peculiar to it: adolescence burns with lust,[40] middle age is rocked by ambition, and old age wastes away in greed[41]—not that everyone is this way, but people are more inclined to these vices according to their age.

16   So we must take care that our young people are kept pure for as long as possible, for premature sexual activity weakens both bodily and mental strength.[42] This will be possible if they are kept from dances and other diversions of this type and likewise from all association with women, or if they say or hear nothing about such matters. For since they are carried along by the fever of their young years toward venery, there will be no hope at all if a bad companion joins their counsels. Success is most likely if they are never allowed holidays. They should always be kept occupied with some honorable physical or mental activity, for leisure makes young people inclined to lust and every intemperance. So when our young people work at what is very much for their welfare, their hard work will be conducive to their well-being. But not only is leisure very dangerous to them, but also solitude, which caresses a weak mind with constant thoughts about such things and prevents it from finding diversion elsewhere. For just as those who are gripped by despair should never be entrusted to solitude,[43] neither should those whose minds have been bound fast by pleasure.

17   So they must also be prohibited and carefully protected from all filth and vile wickedness. They should only be entrusted to

those whose character and entire life has been thoroughly scruti-
nized, who do not present an example leading to sin but possess
the authority to deter them from it. For as stakes are bound to
young treeshoots to prevent them being bent over by their own
weight or by the wind, so also young people should depend on
companions from whose advice they may learn, by whose con-
science they may be restrained, and in imitation of whom they
may improve themselves.[44] The young must also be kept within
limits, lest they become more intemperate with respect to the
other things which surround them in life. For excess food and
drink and sleeping too much come mostly from habit. This is not
to say that the quantity of these needs should not be adapted to
various bodily states, but it is generally true that nature is content
with little support, if we look to necessity; if we look to pleasure,
nothing can ever satisfy her.[45]

At that age especially they should be kept away from wine;   18
drinking too much of it is injurious to good health and greatly dis-
turbs moral reasoning.[46] In this matter the practice of the Spartans seems to me by no means objectionable: they took pains to
have drunken slaves put on show at their banquets — not, indeed,
to take pleasure in their crude talk or filthy behavior (for taking pleasure in the defects or vices of another human being is inhuman), but in
order to show their young men by example how base it is to be seen
drunk.[47] Children, therefore, should drink so that they become accustomed from their earliest years more to the moderation of water than
the frenzy of wine, and they should drink so soberly and frugally that
drink seems to be given more for softening food than slaking thirst. For
it is not proper to fill the stomach with food or drink, or to sleep
through winter nights, or to make satiety the limit of pleasure — this
not only inhibits virtue, but also good health. But it is proper to re-
strain all things by reason,[48] and to get used to reining in the im-
pulses of youth with ease, and to deciding that it is not appropriate to do everything that one's ability or the occasion allows.[49]

19   Above all, however, it is proper for a well-educated youth to respect and practice religion and to be steeped in religious belief
from his earliest youth. For what human thing will be worthy of
respect to one who holds the divine in contempt? It is not proper,
however, to be carried away into old wives' tales, something which
in youth is generally much condemned and lays one open to scorn.
A fixed measure should be observed. To be sure, a measure is hard
to apply where the best we are capable of will fall short of that
measure. But they are to be warned particularly not to utter curses
against holy things, nor to hold up sacred names to scorn — an
abomination at every age — nor to swear lightly of their own accord, for those who swear rashly usually swear often.[50]

20   Next, they should treat the elderly and those who are older than
they with profound reverence, and consider them to be almost in
the position of parents. In this respect, tradition taught Roman youth
well: they used to lead the senators, whom they called "fathers,"
into the senate-house on the day when the senate was convened, and
they waited in regular attendance before the doors, and after the senate had been dismissed, they led them home again in a throng —
these things being, of course, the basic forms of constancy and patience due those of advanced age.[51] Indeed, young men who freely
associate with the elderly and are reluctant to leave those who can
profit them, are clearly the ones who have a steady desire to excel
their contemporaries in virtue. They should be taught, furthermore,
how to welcome visitors suitably and to bid them farewell when they
depart; to greet their elders in a modest way, assemble their juniors in a kindly way, and meet their friends and well-wishers in a
congenial way. Although these things sit well in all young men,
they seem particularly attractive in princes and their children. They
are especially noticed in those in whose manner and entire life ac-
cessibility is usually loved but gravity praised. Nevertheless in the
case of both qualities one should be careful that the latter quality
not turn into rustic harshness or the former into vulgar frivolity.

Good results like these can be achieved if every student is ready   21
to let himself be criticized and admonished, a principle which is
salutary in every age, circumstance and condition. For as we recognize the flaws in our face when a mirror is put before us, so also
we weigh carefully our own mental lapses when our friends up-
braid us, which is the first step to amendment. What is more,
people who won't listen to anything they dislike are the ones most
vulnerable to deception: the weak stomach is one that will only accept delicacies. So it is seemly to endure abuse and listen to chastisement,[52] for those who cannot bear criticism in their presence
are harder to defend in their absence. But it is proper especially for
those who are more fortunate and in whose hands rests authority
over cities and peoples to listen graciously, even willingly, to those
who give them good advice — the more so as their great freedom of
action makes them more inclined toward sin and their sins generally cause harm to many people. And indeed, this is a greater
cause for concern in that there are few who dare tell them what is
right and true,[53] and fewer who want to hear it; for someone who
wishes to hear the truth can easily find someone from whom he
may hear it. So it can seem like a miracle if anyone born into a
powerful position and great good fortune, who has never experienced adversity, turns out to be wise and good; and if there is any
such person, I think he should be loved and worshipped, as it
were, like a god on earth. For between the abundance of things
supplying every pleasure, the power to get whatever they want, and
the huge crowd of flatterers who generally make madmen out of
fools, there is hardly any room for sound reason or right judgment.[54] Plato understood this beautifully and put it into a few
well-chosen words, a passage we should quote here word-for-word
from the *Gorgias:* "It is difficult," he says, "and worthy of great
praise to have lived justly amidst great freedom to sin."[55]

But excessive parental leniency has generally softened and ener-   22
vated young people,[56] which is, as a rule, manifest in those who

have been brought up in luxury under widowed mothers. So the custom among certain nations of taking care that their children are brought up either outside their city, or at any rate among relatives and friends outside the home, is an attractive one. For even if the children generally find these relatives and friends too lenient, nevertheless the fact that they understand themselves to be living in someone else's home makes them less unruly and more inclined toward the better studies that we call liberal. It is now time for us to discuss these studies.

What Liberal Studies Are: A General Treatment

23   We call those studies liberal, then, which are worthy of a free [*liber*] man: they are those through which virtue and wisdom are either practiced or sought, and by which the body or mind is disposed towards all the best things. From this source people customarily seek honor and glory, which for the wise man are the principle rewards of virtue.[57] Just as profit and pleasure are laid down as ends for illiberal intellects, so virtue and glory are goals for the noble.

24   It is therefore fitting to aim for these from the start of infancy and to strive for wisdom with all one's zeal.[58] For if no one can achieve excellence in any of the private arts, even those that require less intellectual ability, without applying one's self to them from earliest youth, what shall we conclude in the case of wisdom, which is relevant to so many great issues and contains the precepts and guiding principles of our entire life? For without question we will not be—insofar as we wish both to be wise and to be regarded as such—we will not be, I say, wise in old age unless we have first begun to be wise in youth. Nor indeed should we accept the common opinion which everybody repeats, and believe that

those who are intelligent beyond their years in their youth eventually tend to lose their mental edge after they have become older. In certain respects, to be sure, this is not incompatible with our understanding of the human body: the senses flourish in childhood, then wither with advancing age. In this regard there is good reason for a certain old man to have been silenced by a young man—the name of each, however, is unknown. For when the young man was considered wise and virtuous beyond his years and was shown to the old man as a prodigy, the old man said, "one who is so wise in his youth will inevitably be senile in his old age"—saying this with his voice raised so that the young man might hear. But the young man forgot none of his inborn shrewdness and immediately turned toward him, saying, "So you must have been remarkably wise in your youth"—running him through with his own weapons, as they say.[59]

Indeed, there is also by nature in many young men such quickness of understanding and such shrewdness in inquiry that, even without much formal learning, they are able to speak about the most important subjects and utter the weightiest opinions. And if their inborn power is strengthened by knowledge and aided by learning, this education will generally produce the greatest men.[60] So we must take diligent care of men like these, but not neglect those of average intellect; rather we must help them the more in that their natural ability falls short. Nevertheless all of them are to be bound over to their studies and labors from childhood,

> while young minds are malleable, while they are young enough
> to change,[61]

as Vergil's verse goes.

We must, then, press onwards the more as that time of life is better suited to learning[62] than other times, yet we should learn at every age[63]—unless there is a time when learning is more shameful than ignorance! The contrary judgment was expressed by Cato, the head of the Porcius family, who learned Latin letters on the threshold of old age and Greek when he was quite old; he did not believe it degrading for an old man to learn what is fine for any man to know.[64] Even so great a philosopher as Socrates applied himself to the lyre when he was already advanced in years and turned over his fingers to a teacher for guidance.[65] Meanwhile, our young people, for God's sake, are too lazy and soft to learn, and feel ashamed to be subject to a teacher though they have scarcely been weaned! But they are not to be left to their own judgment; they must be induced through various devices to undertake a good and principled course of studies.

27   Some must be snared by praise and the attractions of honor; others by little gifts and compliments; still others must be compelled by threats and floggings.[66] And indeed all these arts must be so correctly weighed and reasonably controlled that teachers may vary their use even in the case of the selfsame mind, and care must be taken that they be neither too indulgent toward their students nor too harsh. For just as excessive freedom unhinges innate good qualities, so harsh, unrelenting criticism saps intellectual energies and quenches the little fires that nature lights in children. Boys who fear everything will dare nothing,[67] and it is the case that boys who are afraid of making mistakes in every single thing will make mistakes always. Above all, those who abound in black bile should be controlled more loosely, and it is a good idea to give them their head to enjoy freedom and fun. Not all (as Aristotle would have it), but certainly a great many clever people have this sort of complexion.[68]

28   But it happens that a great many of those endowed with a noble intellect, while they are striving to follow the right course of studies, are called back under compulsion; or as a result of certain bars, as it were, set across their path, they are forced to stop in mid-course or are sidetracked into another one. For a great many students, limited family resources have been the impediment

which constrained a noble mind, born for better things, to enslave itself to the pursuit of gain. Yet a noble nature generally rises above the greatest difficulties, and great material wealth usually injures good minds more than the most abject poverty. Of such men it is generally said, not without some resentment: "O how great this man would have been, if he had been born in lesser circumstances!" For some, the authority of parents and childhood habits stand in the way, for we follow seamlessly as adults the habits we have formed as children, and boys willingly let themselves be shaped by the desires of the parents who have given them birth and brought them up. But we also generally follow the customary practices of our cities, as though what others approve of and do is necessarily the best course [for us]. So this kind of decision is the most difficult of all, for either it is not a free decision, or we come to it only after being steeped in false opinions derived from bad customs and the corrupt conversation of mankind.

Nevertheless there are some to whom the ability has been given 29 as a singular gift of God to enter and stick to the right way by themselves, without any guide[69] — "to those few," and the ones "whom" (as the poet says) "favoring Jove loved," or even begat,[70] to give mythology its due. We understand that Hercules in particular was like this, as the Greeks relate and the Romans after them recalled. He saw before him two paths, one of virtue and the other of pleasure, and being, as it happened, at the age when one must choose one's way for all of life, he withdrew into a solitary place. There, by himself, he thought long and hard (judgment and discernment being weak at that age), and after rejecting pleasure, he at last embraced virtue. From that time forth he made a path to heaven for himself via many formidable labors, according to human belief. So much, then, for him. For ourselves it is a good outcome whether we are led to virtue by the hand of precept[71] or compelled thereto by force and necessity; and fortunate indeed is the necessity that drives one to the good.

The Finest Studies: Arms and Letters

30 To be sure, I see that this has happened in some measure to you, Ubertino, as well. For among the studies and liberal arts of mankind are two in particular that have the greatest affinity with cultivating virtue and obtaining glory, namely, instruction in letters and arms. And although through the indulgence of your father you were allowed to pursue only the latter, which is almost the private preserve of your family, you have embraced both with such tenacious diligence and zeal that you have left your contemporaries far behind and are able to compete with your elders in both species of renown. You therefore do well in not neglecting the art of war, in which your ancestors have always excelled, and in attempting to add new renown in letters to your family's old glory in arms.

31   For you are not eager to imitate those (of whom there is a large crowd in our times) who shrink from the reputation of being learned, as though it were something shameful, nor do you approve of the opinion of Licinius, the old Roman emperor, who used to call letters a poison and a public plague.[72] States would be far more blessed, Plato says, if philosophers ruled or if their rulers happened to be philosophers.[73] To be sure, it is true that the disciplines of letters take away neither madness nor wickedness. But they are a great help to those who were born for virtue and wisdom, and they often provide the means for uncovering stupidity or more destructive kinds of wrongdoing. For we know that Claudius (to stick with Roman emperors) was quite learned, and it is an established fact that Nero, his stepson and successor as emperor, was particularly well-educated;[74] of these two, the former was notoriously deranged and the latter was steeped in cruelty and all the vices. Nevertheless, Nero once said, on the pretext of showing mercy, that he wished he were unlettered.[75] But if he could have been merciful in some other way besides illiteracy, surely he would

have wished for that! But in my view, if he had been allowed to cast letters aside, which were ill-suited to his character, he would have done so with the same readiness and enthusiasm with which he stripped away that feigned and temporary clemency, so as to leave no room in himself for any of the virtues or liberal arts.[76] By way of contrast, Giacomo da Carrara, your ancestor, a prudent man and a generous prince but not himself very learned, nevertheless cultivated learned men wondrously, and held that this one thing had been lacking to his good fortune, that he was not educated to the extent that a modest man might wish to be.

One may wish to be learned in old age, but it is not easy to achieve this unless we have nurtured learning in ourselves from our earliest years with zealous effort. So we need to prepare in youth those consolations which can bring delight in honorable old age; studies which are burdensome to youth will be pleasant relaxations to age. In this sense they are truly great bulwarks, whether we seek a remedy against sloth or solace in the face of worry and care.[77] For there are two kinds of life befitting a free man, one consisting entirely in leisure and contemplation, the other in action and business.[78] It can escape no one that the knowledge and use of writing is very necessary to the former kind of life; and in the latter their utility can easily be discerned from the following argument. To say nothing of how much wiser they can become from the precepts of literary authorities as well as from the example of those about whom books are written, men of action can have no more pleasant relaxation when they are tired, whether they engage in affairs of state or foreign wars or whether they busy themselves with their own affairs and those of their friends. Also, when times and moments arise when it is necessary to withdraw from the active life — for we are often unwillingly prevented from participating in affairs of state, and wars are not always being waged, and particular days and nights offer occasions when it is fitting to stay at home and be by one's self — at such times, then, when we may not

.32

take part in outdoor diversions, reading and books will come to our assistance. That is, unless we want to indulge ourselves utterly with sleep and rot with indolence, or imitate the custom of the emperor Domitian, who every day at a fixed time went off by himself and chased flies with an iron stylus.[79] He was the son of Vespasian and the younger brother of Titus, but without question he was far from being their equal. Indeed, he was considered the most repulsive of the emperors as Titus is thought to be the most virtuous of all (Titus being he whom the histories call the "darling of humankind"[80]). Thus the reputation of Titus is as celebrated as that of Domitian is detested.

33   The fact is that posterity is free in its judgment of the lives and affairs of mankind; it does not shrink from condemning the wicked, nor does it begrudge praise to those who deserve it. In this respect it is, as we see, a great prerogative of princes — indeed, I might almost say it is a necessity set before them — to act well if they value the judgment of mankind and a lasting reputation among posterity. Other, more humble men need great energy and strength of character to emerge into the light [of fame], and their sins are hidden by the obscurity of their lot.[81] In princes and great men, however, virtue — either because it is rare amidst good fortune and therefore more greatly admired, or because it gleams more brightly from fortune's splendor — virtue, even modest virtue, is considered remarkable and renowned; whereas evil deeds cannot remain hidden, even secret ones, nor can silence be long preserved once they become known. For the very men who minister to their pleasures, the very companions and witnesses of their crimes, bring them into the open and are the first to condemn them. An example is the witty jest one of Domitian's intimate servants used to censure the emperor's lunatic behavior, for when he was once asked whether anyone was inside with Domitian, he answered, "not even a fly,"[82] as though the emperor had wiped them all out with his stylus.

One might perhaps forgive Domitian for this indecorous form 34
of hunting if only it were established what he got up to when
alone during the winter,[83] or if he had not deserved hatred for his
foul crimes much more than mockery for his repulsive fly-hunts.
For what Scipio used to say about himself—that he was never less
alone or at leisure than when he seemed to be so[84]—cannot happen to just anyone, but only to those endowed with great intellects
and outstanding virtue. Even though that man seems to me in no
way inferior who is able to preserve his solitude even in a crowd
and his tranquillity in the midst of business affairs. This was in
fact written of Cato, who, while the senate was being called into
session, used to pore over books in the senate-house.[85] No doubt
this was why he habitually offered highly beneficial advice to his
country concerning both current affairs and matters of permanent
importance.

Yet if literary study offered no other reward—and its rewards 35
are certainly numerous and great—the distraction it offers from
the many things we cannot bring to mind without disgracing ourselves or remember without causing ourselves pain ought in any
case to make it quite valuable enough. For if there is anything either in ourselves or our fortune that causes us discomfort, we are
easily relieved of it for this reason: that the pursuit of knowledge
gives birth to wondrous pleasures in the human mind and in due
course bears the richest fruits, whenever a seed of this kind falls
into a good mind that is suited to nurture it. Therefore when we
are alone and free from all our other cares, what better thing can
we do than resort to our books, where everything is either most
agreeable for learning or most conducive to living a good, holy
life?[86]

For although written records are very valuable indeed for other 36
purposes, they are especially valuable for preserving the memory of
the past, as they contain the deeds of mankind, the unhoped-for
turns of fortune, the unusual works of nature, and (more impor-

tant than all these things) the guiding principles of historical periods. For human memory and objects passed from hand to hand gradually decay and scarcely survive the lifetime of one person, but what has been skillfully entrusted to books endures forever. Perhaps a picture or carven marble or cast metal can excel even a well-written book, but such objects do not describe the times, nor do they readily disclose motivation in all its variety; they only express exterior states and fall easily into ruin. What is preserved in literary form, however, not only renders speech but also distinguishes styles of speaking and represents people's thoughts. And if it has been published in numerous copies, it cannot easily perish, provided its diction is distinguished. For whatever is written in an undistinguished way is not given credibility and cannot long endure.

37   What way of life, then, can be more delightful, or indeed more beneficial, than to read and write all the time: for moderns to understand things ancient; for present generations to converse with their posterity; and thus to make every time our own, both past and future? What excellent furniture books make! as we say; and as Cicero says, What a happy family books make![87] Absolutely honest and well-behaved! A family that does not fuss or shout, that is neither rapacious, voracious or contumacious, that speaks or remains silent as it is bidden, that always stands ready to execute your every command, and that you never hear saying anything you don't want to hear, and that only says as much as you want to hear.

38   So, since our memory cannot hold everything and indeed retains very little, scarcely enough for particular purposes, books, in my view, should be acquired and preserved as a kind of second memory. For letters and books constitute a fixed record of things and are the communal repository of all things knowable. If by chance we are not able to create anything ourselves, we ought at least to pass on carefully the books we have received from those who have come before us to those who will come after, keeping

them whole and uncorrupted, and in this manner we will usefully serve the interests of posterity and give past generations at least this one recompense for their labors. In this respect we can perhaps find fault with a certain age and the ages that followed them; we may even become aggrieved, though profitlessly, that they allowed so many remarkable works of famous authors to perish. Of some of these we have the names alone (though embellished with high praises); in the case of other authors, parts and fragments have come down to us. That is why we long so for their works: from the famous names and the renown they have won. The excellence and value of what yet survives makes the loss of the rest hard to endure, even though we have received much of their surviving works in such a badly corrupted, mutilated and mangled state that it would almost have been better if nothing of them had survived.

But not the least part of this great loss must seem the many things worthy of note that have been done in Italy, now largely hidden from us, knowledge of which has perished with the books and records of them. Thus we know the deeds of the barbarians, but are ignorant of much of our own history thanks to the plight of books. And so it has come about that we seek reliable knowledge even of Roman history from Greek authors, for a great many things but sparingly recorded in Latin writers, or completely unknown to them, are found widely diffused in Greek authors, although the [ancient] Greek language, which at one time our ancestors used to speak as though it was their mother tongue,[88] has almost died out among its own people, and among us Latin-speakers is thoroughly extinct, except for a certain few people who in this age have applied themselves to it, and now are bringing it from the tomb back to life.[89]

But I return to history, whose loss is the more serious in that knowledge of it is more useful and pleasant. For to the truly noble mind, and to those who are obligated to involve themselves in public affairs and human communities, knowledge of history and

39

40

the study of moral philosophy are the more suitable subjects. The rest of the arts are called liberal because they befit free men, but philosophy is liberal because its study makes men free.[90] Thus in philosophy we find rules explaining what one may profitably do or shun, but in history we find [moral] examples; in the former the duties of all mankind may be found and what it is fitting for each person to do, but in the latter what has been done or said in every age. Unless I am mistaken, a third study should be added to these [in the case of the public man]: eloquence, which is a distinct part of civics.[91] Through philosophy we can acquire correct views, which is of first importance in everything; through eloquence we can speak with weight and polish, which is the one skill that most effectively wins over the minds of the masses; but history helps us with both. For if we consider old people wiser and listen to them gladly because they have found out many things in the course of their long lives both through their own experience and through the other people they have seen and heard, how much ought we to esteem those who have memorized things worth knowing from many centuries and are able to produce an example to illuminate every situation? The outcome of these studies is to enable anyone to speak well and to inspire him to act as well as possible; this is the mark of the greatest men and the absolutely finest characters.

41   There were four things which the Greeks used to teach their boys: letters, wrestling, music, and drawing,[92] which some call sketching. We shall speak of wrestling and music later. Drawing as it is now practiced is not worthy of a free man, except perhaps insofar as it pertains to writing (for penmanship is actually a form of drawing and sketching); for the rest, it is the business of painters. However, among the Greeks, Aristotle tells us, this kind of business was not only useful, but also honorable. For skill in design helped in the the purchase of vases, paintings, and statues, which the Greeks took much pleasure in, and prevented their being deceived about price, and it gave them great appreciation for the

beauty and charm of things both natural and artificial.[93] Great men need to be able to talk among themselves and make judgements about matters of this kind.

The fruits of literature, on the other hand, are always great, for 42 the whole of life and for every kind of person,[94] but it is particularly beneficial to the studious for forming habits [of virtue] and strengthening the memory of times past as well as for the acquisition of learning. From the beginning, therefore, if we want some profit from our studies, we must practice appropriate patterns of speech, and take care that we are not found making embarrassing small slips while pursuing great effects.[95] Next, we must take up the practice of disputation, through which, by supple argument, we seek what is true or false in each and every subject. Disputation is the science of learning and the learning of science, and so opens with ease the way to every kind of knowledge. Rhetoric is third among the rational disciplines; through it one seeks the art of eloquence,[96] which we have also placed third among the principal parts of civics. But although in times gone by it used to be widely studied as part of a nobleman's education, rhetoric has now fallen almost totally into disuse. It has been completely exiled from legal proceedings, where contending parties no longer use long speeches, but rather adduce laws against each other dialectically in support of their cases. In judicial rhetoric many young Romans once achieved great glory, either by denouncing the guilty or defending the innocent. For deliberative rhetoric as well there has been no room among princes and lords for a long time, since they want an opinion explained in few words and arguments brought nakedly into council; while in popular regimes the most brilliant speakers are thought to be those who speak artlessly and at great length. There remains only the demonstrative genus, which, though it has never fallen out of use, is scarcely ever used correctly today.[97] For in making speeches, nearly everyone uses those arts which may be more properly described as contrary to art. In this state of affairs, the one whom we wish to be well educated must nevertheless work at rhetoric, so that in situations appropriate to each genus of rhetoric he can use his art to speak with polish and elaboration.[98]

43   Next comes poetics, which, even if it contributes a great deal to the life and speech of those who study it, nevertheless seems more suited to pleasure.[99] Indeed the art of music, which also delights the listener, was once held in great honor among the Greeks, nor was anyone considered liberally educated unless he knew how to sing and play the lyre. Socrates himself learned these skills as an old man,[100] and enjoined noble youths to acquire them, not to stimulate licentious behavior but to moderate the movements of soul under the rule of reason. For just as not every voice makes a melodious sound, but only one that harmonizes well, so also not all movements of the soul, but only those which accord with reason, contribute to a harmonious life. But inasmuch as the use of musical modes is highly effective in relaxing the mind and calming the passions, knowledge of this subject is indeed worthy of a free mind and provides the principles according to which we theorize concerning the various natures and properties of sounds and their mutual proportions, from which are produced consonances and dissonances.

44   The discipline concerning numbers, called arithmetic, and the one concerning magnitudes, called geometry, are similar. In these disciplines the different species of numbers and magnitudes are established and their many properties are demonstrated in accordance, respectively, with the various relationships among equals and unequals, and among lines, surfaces, and bodies. Knowledge of this sort is most pleasant and contains within itself a high degree of certainty.[101] Another very fine discipline is the one that treats the motions, magnitudes, and distances of the heavenly bodies, for it calls us away from the shadows and murkiness down here and leads the eyes and the mind to that shining home above,

adorned with so many lights. As we gaze upwards, it is pleasant to pick out the constellations of the fixed stars and to note the locations and names of the planets and their conjunctions, and likewise to foresee and foretell far in advance the eclipses of the sun and moon. Indeed, knowledge about nature is especially appropriate to and in conformity with the human intellect, for through this knowledge we understand the principles and processes of natural things, both animate and inanimate, as well as the causes and effects of the motions and transformations of those things which are contained in heaven and on earth, and we are able to explain many things that generally seem miraculous to the vulgar. There is nothing that is not pleasant to understand, but it is especially pleasant to concern ourselves with those things which cause sensible effects in the air and round about the earth. The studies closely related to them, like perspective and systems of weights and measures, are equally attractive subjects for investigation.

Since I have advanced so far in my discourse, let me touch also   45
on the remaining disciplines. Medicine is a very fine thing to know about and very useful for bodily health, but its practice contains very little that is suitable for the noble mind. Skill in the law is useful, both to the community and to the individual, and is held in great honor everywhere; indeed, it is derived from moral philosophy, just as medicine is from natural philosophy. But while it is honorable to explain the law to students, or to be consulted on points of law by litigants, it is unseemly for those who handle cases to try to sell their efforts for a fee or settlement.[102] Divine science[103] concerns the loftiest causes and matters remote from our senses that only intelligence can reach.[104]

We have enumerated almost all the chief disciplines, not in or-   46
der that each person need necessarily understand all of them to the point of being learned, or being considered learned — indeed each discipline could absorb all a man's efforts, and the capacity to be content with modest learning is a virtue just like being content

with modest wealth.[105] We have done this rather so that everyone might embrace the study most suitable to himself—although all studies are so linked together that no one of them can be well understood if the others are completely unknown.[106]

47   However, intellects do differ. Some find readily in any given subject the argument and the middle term to prove their own assertions, while others are slow to find arguments but distinguish judiciously among them. Intellects of the former kind are better at posing arguments, while the latter excel as respondents. Likewise, the former type is suited to poetry and the theoretical sciences, the latter to the empirical sciences. Some are quick-witted, but slow of speech and tongue; such persons seem to be best at prepared speeches and artful orations. On the other hand those who are ready both of mind and speech are excellently suited to dialectical disputations. Those whose speech is quicker than their wit—that is, those who have a ready tongue but a dull mind—excel at neither kind of speaking. Furthermore, in certain people the power of memory is very strong, and these are good at historical investigation and at taking in large law books.[107] In this regard we should know that memory apart from intellect is not worth much, but intellect without memory is worth almost nothing, at least as far as learning disciplines is concerned. Yet such a mind can have value in matters of action, since it is possible to write down things that have been done or must be done to compensate for poor memory. Nevertheless, in the case of book-learning, whatever we do not have by heart or cannot easily recall we seem not to know at all.[108]

48   There are, beyond these, people whose psychic powers are abstracted from sensible and material things, and more suited to understanding immaterial substances and universals; others, by contrast, are prone to run off and busy themselves with particulars. The latter are suited to practical wisdom[109] and natural science, the former to mathematics and to the divine science called meta-

physics. For the rest, people should follow the studies appropriate to their natural bent, as the intellect may be speculative or practical. In addition, there are certain limited intellects, the cloddish sort, as the lawyers say, which although they are feeble-minded in everything else, nevertheless have one or another outstanding talent. They should be allowed to do only what they are judged most capable of doing.[110] Aristotle, indeed, being concerned with the active, civic life, believed one should not over-indulge in the liberal arts nor linger over them in pursuit of perfection.[111] For someone who dedicates himself completely to theory and the delights of literature perchance becomes dear to himself, but whether a prince or a private citizen, he is surely of little use to his city.[112]

Such are the definitions we need to make concerning disciplines and intellectual abilities and the genera of both. In this respect it must be observed, to begin with, that it is beneficial to learn from the best masters not only the more important rules that are taught to advanced students, but the first elements of the arts as well. Nor should we spend our time dipping into just any authors; we should read the best. For this reason even Philip, king of Macedon, wanted Alexander to learn his first lessons from Aristotle,[113] and the old Romans took care that when they turned their children over to a school, they were first educated in Vergil. Both had the best of reasons. For what has been sown in young minds puts down deep roots and there is no force that can afterwards pull it up again.[114] Hence, if they become accustomed to the best [teachers and authors] from the beginning, they will use and possess them always as their paramount authorities and guides. But if they imbibe any errors, twice as much time will be needed: to shake out errors, and then to inculcate true precepts. That is why Timotheus, a famous musician of his time, who was exiled from Sparta because he had increased the number of strings on the lyre and invented new musical modes, required a fixed fee from stu-

49

dents who had not begun their studies under other teachers, but demanded double from those who had learned something from others.[115]

50   In the process of learning, the very thing that ought to be a great help, namely, a great desire to learn, often becomes for many people an impediment. They want to take in everything at the same time, and are able to retain nothing as a result. For as excess food does not nourish, but disgusts the stomach, weighing down and weakening the rest of the body, so a great abundance of things ingested all at once into the memory slips away heedlessly now and weakens the memory for the future. So always let those who are eager to learn read widely, but let them select a few things each day that their memory can digest, and in this way let them store away three or four things or more, as each one's ability or leisure will allow, as the special profit of that day. By reading other things, they will succeed in preserving by meditation what they have already learned and daily reading will make more familiar to them what they have yet to master.

51   What is more, this excessive desire to know and learn is generally joined with a certain disorderly curiosity to investigate. For when people like this are eager to take up many things one by one, they fall upon the various disciplines all at once, going back now to this one, now to that; now they embrace one subject with all their strength, then, having cast that aside, they embrace another for a bit, then another. This is not only completely useless, but even very damaging, for there is truth in the proverb which says: wines turn sour when they are rebottled too often. So it is better to devote oneself to one thing and to pursue it with all one's zeal, and to try to grasp the disciplines in the order they were transmitted by their authors. For those who read books in a disorderly way, now beginning from the end, now dipping into the middle, learning second what they should have learned first—the only profit such people take from their reckless reading is the appearance of

having read nothing at all. And we should familiarize ourselves with the numerous books within the same discipline so as always to have the better ones foremost.[116]

Not everyone should undertake the same amount of labor, but each according to his turn of mind. For some minds penetrate like lead (so to speak), others like iron. Leaden minds that are blunt are not much good for learning, while those whose mental edge is sharp but soft and easily bent require frequent breaks in their studying. If they do not penetrate through to their goal with the first blow, they grow blunter the more they try. But nothing is impervious to those who been allotted an intellect of iron, if it is also sharp, unless they want to penetrate an unbreakable barrier. If they have blunt iron minds, they can still prevail over all difficulties through diligent effort. Hence if they do not understand something, they do not spit it out immediately like the proud, nor do they fall into despair, like the weak of will; they simply persevere the more in their intention. But it is also very true that those who are keener in mind are less strong in memory, and those who grasp things quickly retain fewer of them.[117] So in order to preserve and strengthen memory, the plan Cato said he used is especially germane: he used to call to mind in the evening whatever he had done, seen, or read during the day,[118] as though demanding an account of the day's business from himself, like someone who wanted to take account not only of his business activities, but also of his leisure. So we shall therefore, if we are able, take care to remember everything. If we cannot, let us at least cling tenaciously to the things we have chosen for ourselves as especially important.

It will moreover be profitable to confer often with our classmates about our common studies, for disputation sharpens the mind, educates the tongue, and strengthens the memory, and not only do we learn numerous things through disputation, but we also understand better, express more aptly, and remember more firmly the things we learn this way.[119] But also, by teaching others

52

53

what we learn, we will be of no small help to ourselves; teaching what you have learned is the best way to improve.[120] However it happens to almost all learners, when they make good progress in something at first, that they immediately think they have achieved great things in the disciplines and would dispute already as though they were learned men and would defend their own opinions strenuously, which is a great obstacle to them. For the first step in learning is the capacity to doubt, nor is there anything so inimical to learning as the presumption of one's own erudition or excessive reliance upon one's own wits: the one takes away our interest in learning, while the other diminishes it, and in this way students unnecessarily deceive themselves. The easiest person to deceive is one's self, and there is no one our deceit damages more than ourselves. This comes about because inexperienced students have not yet been permitted to assess the byways, bends and precipices which lie hidden in the sciences; hence they either mistakenly correct many things in books which they they are unable to understand well on their own, or they blame the ignorance and carelessness of scribes, passing deliberately over the numerous things they do not understand. Effort and perseverance will shrug off such attitudes, however.

54   Everything will happen satisfactorily if time will be apportioned suitably, if every day we allot fixed times to letters and are not distracted by affairs of any kind from reading something every day. For if Alexander used to read a great deal while campaigning,[121] if Caesar used to write books even while marching with his army, and Augustus, after having undertaken so great an affair as the Modenese war, nevertheless always read or wrote in camp and declaimed every day,[122] what activity is there that could interrupt *our* citified leisure-hours and summon us for so long from our literary studies? Moreover it is useful to regard the loss of even the least bit of time as significant and to account for our time like our life and our health, so that we do not lose anything needlessly,[123] just

as when we allot our moments of inactivity, which others use for leisure, to less strenuous studies or pass such times in pleasant reading. And indeed there is good reason also to assemble those good moments that others usually neglect, as when someone reads at table and falls asleep (or escapes sleep) reading. True, doctors claim these things harm the vision and the eyes, but this is only the case if one reads excessively, that is, either too intently or after a heavy meal. But this, too, would be of no small profit: if inside our libraries we should set up right before our eyes those devices which are used to measure the hours and times, so that we may see time glide away, as it were; and if we should use those places for no other purpose than that for which they have been established, and allow there no extraneous thoughts or activities.

On Physical Exercises and Military Pursuits

Let these words be heeded with greater zeal and attention by those who have minds more fit for learning than bodies fit for war. Those, however, who have both vigorous minds and strong bodies ought to pay attention to both pursuits, shaping their mind so that it can discern the truth and will reason's commands, and their body so that it can endure with fortitude and obey with ease. Finally, we ought to prepare ourselves in every way to prevent injustice rather than inflict violence, or, if it should be allowable to use force, we should not fight for the sake of plunder or greed, but for command and glory.[124] It is, indeed, highly appropriate for princes to learn military discipline, for they should be well provisioned with the arts of peace and war, and should be able to lead armies and fight physically themselves when necessary. Alexander the Great used often to indicate this obligation in words, as he always did in deed: for whenever a dispute would arise, as it was liable to, among his friends as to which of Homer's verses was the

55

choicest, Alexander (who was extremely fond of Homer) used always to prefer one verse in particular about Agamemnon:

both a good king and a powerful warrior

as though saying that it is a seemly thing for the same man who is a good king also to be a brave fighter.[125]

56   The body, then, should be trained from its very infancy for military service and the mind should be shaped for endurance. As we do with horses, we should lead young persons by the hand into the arena, so that they may become accustomed to bear with ease the sun and toil amid dust and sweat. For just as we often see thin little tree branches bearing a great weight of apples that have grown from their flower to full size, bending but not breaking under the weight — a weight that would knock down even stronger branches if it had not increased insensibly — so in the case of human beings. Unless from childhood and through all the stages of life they harden both mind and body to endure toil, they will immediately be broken and unable to resist if afterwards any danger should threaten them. It is this very hardening that the authority of Minos and Lycurgus, the celebrated legislators of antiquity, enjoins. The laws of the Cretans and Spartans trained their youth in exercises designed not only for physical endurance but also for mental self-control. They directed their young, who were brought up outside the home, to engage in hunting. In this way youths practiced running and jumping, and learned to endure hunger and thirst, cold and heat,[126] capacities they could easily turn to military use. For luxuries weaken the human mind and body, but toil strengthens and hardens them. Unless they are hardened to toil, they will not be able to stand it, but those accustomed to the effortless use of mind and body will undergo when necessary all dangers and difficulties.

57   In this regard I am able to place no more illustrious example before you, either from the ancients or from our contemporaries,

than that of your father. For as you yourself see, I willingly place before you the images of your ancestors and I often devote myself to recalling them to your memory, since they possess a certain magnificence that you would do well to follow, and people are generally more inspired by examples from their own homes. For just as it is glorious to surpass one's own family in benefaction, so it is generally thought shameful to degenerate in the way we live and in our habits from those whose virtue gives us honor.

But to return to your father. He can be praised for countless things, but he himself nevertheless usually glories most in his capacity for toil. As we see, he is so tireless in his efforts and so audacious in peril that he seems to think he possesses a weightless body or that he belongs to no mortal race.[127] Indeed, his contempt for toil gives birth to contempt for death as well, and increases his audacity. So intrepidly does he approach every difficulty that one must believe he fears nothing—except, perhaps, the possibility that he might die an old man. This seems to me an excellent attitude. We should always look to virtue and turn our mind upon famous deeds; we should not care overmuch for life.[128] Whoever will weigh worldly things at their true value will readily see that the fruits of a long life are fewer than would justify expending great effort to seek them, and that the mischances of life are greater than would justify hoping for even a brief life. It is fitting, then, that one who lives honorably in peace and acts bravely in war should bear all things with equanimity and accept death calmly, whenever it comes, even hastening to meet it when circumstance or necessity demands.

For we ought not to fear that we have perchance lived too little, but rather that we have lived too little of the life we *have* lived.[129] Every period of life has the capacity to yield something splendid. Scipio, who afterwards was the first to be called Africanus, was barely an adolescent when he served his country under his father against the Carthaginians. When Hannibal crushed the Romans

58

59

by the river Ticino, Scipio saved from peril his own father, the consul and commander, who had been seriously wounded and surrounded by the enemy. Thus the boy Scipio, by his faithful and brave action, saved a consul, a general, a citizen and a father from a battle that veterans were hardly able to escape, and thus deservedly earned praise for both his public and private merits.[130] Aemilius Lepidus, too, was sent into battle as a boy, and in the same encounter both killed an enemy and saved a citizen; in his memory a statue of him wearing the *toga praetexta* was set up on the Capitoline by decree of the senate, so that others also might be inspired by his example and so that honor might be paid to the author of so famous a youthful accomplishment.[131] But let us not begrudge you your own praises. You, too, though younger than either of them,[132] while at Brescia recently in the army of the Germans, dared to march in arms against the enemy, when none of the other soldiers would volunteer so much. I hardly know whether your deed aroused greater wonder among your enemies or shame among your friends.[133]

60   Children, then, should be taught from their first years the capacity to dare great things and endure difficulties. And what about those Spartan children? The ancients used to praise them a great deal for the care taken in their education. It was customary for them to show such great endurance in contests with their contemporaries that when they had been thrown down violently or had fallen down by chance in the middle of a struggle, they allowed themselves to be killed or to expire rather than admit defeat. *That* custom must have put some spirit in them! Are we surprised at this, when even at an altar[134] they used to receive such beatings that a great deal of blood always flowed, and often they even expired? Yet no one ever either cried out or gave the least sign of pain.[135] Being thus trained at home, their young men in the end performed those military exploits that fill the memory of all antiquity. What, indeed, might they hear from either their general or

their fathers that could equal the blandishments they heard from their mothers, who told them, as they were about to march against the enemy, to bring their weapons back if they lived, or be brought back on them if they died?[136] Since they believed that surrendering their arms to the enemy or throwing them away in flight was worse than death, they would care for their weapons and protect them as though they were parts of their body. No wonder they used to offer themselves to view in their armor while living, when they believed that to bring back one's armor was a mark of honor even for the dead! Their custom and practice of bearing arms was so outstanding that they used their arms like limbs or clothing, which seemed to add no weight to their bodies. If the Roman legions had not been trained by long and assiduous practice (and the word for army, *exercitus*, comes from practice, *exercere*), how could they ever have marched with their infantry in a column and borne their arms, often on the run, as well as defensive stakes, and anything else they needed for daily use, and often, on top of that, food for fifteen days or more — a hard burden for a mule?[137]

Therefore those who are to be dedicated to the study of either 61 arms or letters (these being the most liberal and the most important of the arts, because they are most suited to princes) as soon as age will permit them to use their limbs, ought to accustom themselves to arms; and they should be charged with learning their first letters as soon as they can form words. Immediately thereafter they should get a foretaste of the activities and studies they will pursue throughout life, and practice their rudiments. Both of these activities they can easily pursue by turns, so they will have fixed hours for bodily exercises and, likewise, fixed hours set apart for literary exercises. And it is fitting that not only boys, but also men do this. It was a practice attributed even to the emperor Theodosius, who by day would engage in military exercises or render legal judgements concerning the affairs of his subjects, but by night would apply himself to his books by lamplight.[138] But con-

cerning literary studies we have given our views at more than sufficient length above; so let us go on to what remains.

62   Those exercises, then, should be undertaken which preserve
good health and render the limbs more robust; here the natural
disposition of each must be constantly kept in mind, for those
whose physical condition is soft and moist must be dried and
hardened by vigorous exercise, but others will require less, and it is
best for those whose blood is easily inflamed to rest quietly when
the sun is hot. But also age must be taken into account, so that up
until the age of puberty they should be subjected to lighter burdens, lest the sinews be worn down, even at this age, or the growth
of the body impeded.[139] But after puberty they should be broken
to heavier tasks; and it is more appropriate in the case of children
to educate their minds, while older youths should receive education in character. Likewise, with children the concern should be
with discipline, while with adolescents one should take greater
care over the body's strength and health.[140]

63   The importance of youthful exercises and the care that must be
devoted to them is exemplified by Marius. Plutarch attests that
when he was an old man and very heavy in the body, this great
war-hero, even though it was peacetime, went every day to the military camp with the young men and exercised with them in order
to teach his son the duties and actions of a soldier.[141] Thanks to
these make-believe contests they go off to real battles with greater
courage and skill. If this instruction in fighting that is so sought
after in peace and at leisure were not useful, then it was in vain
that the wise consul Publius Rutilius was the first to order his
troops to receive training in the handling of arms. He summoned
the most skillful gladiators from the city and commanded that
their method of avoiding and inflicting blows be introduced into
the camps, so that his soldiers might be proficient not only in
strength and courage (which was all that he aimed at previously)
but also in drilling and technique.[142]

So young men should be taught things relevant to this practice, 64
such as the ability to strike the enemy with a sword in their right
hand and cover themselves with a small shield in their left; to
handle sword, spit, club, and lance in either hand; and now to
throw [missiles], now to hide beneath their shields; and to strike
with the point and edge of their weapons without difficulty. They
should practice running, jumping, and wrestling; hold boxing
matches; practice throwing javelins as far as possible; shoot arrows
accurately; swing pikes; roll rocks; and break in horses, now urging them to run and jump by digging in the spurs, now turning
them into a gallop by relaxing the reins. They should prepare
themselves in both sorts of exercises so that every one of them can
fight easily both as a knight and a footsoldier. A tournament of
knights in which they attack one another with hostile lances generally makes them more audacious and skilled in battle, as they
learn to put their own spearpoints where they aim them and to endure a charging line of battle with steady gaze.

The kinds of arms and how they are used, like clothing, change 65
daily; it will be well to follow these changes and try each of them,
but always stick to the better ones. Similarly, battle tactics are constantly changing. Once, in the times of the old heroes, command-
ers used to fight in chariots. Later, particularly with the Romans,
there were few knights (or at least not many); the power of an
army rested entirely with its infantry. Now no one fights in chariots, and almost everyone fights on horseback.

But it is good to keep current usage, so long as it is successful, 66
and to practice it assiduously in campaign exercises; in the end,
soldiers should have training in all kinds of fighting. For things are
done one way in a melee; another when the decision rests entirely
on a battle formation; another when there is an infantry charge,
and another when the conflict takes the form of a duel. (Most
men who seem exceedingly brave fighting in a battle line lose their
strength and spirit when summoned to single combat.) To be

sure, this kind of training which takes the form of games is very different from what one learns in the tumult of battle, when everything is wanting and fear is real. Thus Horace warns,

> O friend, let a healthy boy learn to endure
> the confines of poverty in severe military service,
> and let the cavalryman who inspires fear
> pursue the fierce Parthians with his spear,
> and let him pass his life under the open sky
> and in fearful affairs.[143]

For in this way he will arrive at those more important things that future generals must acquire by thought and practice, such as the arts of leading an army, where camps should be pitched, in what order battle lines should be positioned, how one can anticipate enemy plans and lay ambushes for them (as is customary in battle) while avoiding their ambushes, how to scatter the soldiers of a hostile army but hold one's own soldiers together by fear and kindness, and how to keep military discipline tight.

67 For as the valor of soldiers generally yields praise for generals, so also their failings are generally blamed on the general. Indeed, the glory that comes from good deeds is unequal to the shame that comes from mistakes. The general should execute everything as he planned it for the occasion, and not be thrown into confusion as though by new and unforeseen events. The courage of soldiers cannot stand where the planning of their general fails. Soldiers themselves should be naturally brave and trained in the arts of warfare; they should have plenty of spirit, sufficient arms, and no more nourishment than is strictly necessary. Experience and practice will teach the roles of the general and the soldier as well as the duties of the knight and the infantryman. It is widely repeated that these things are better learned from practice than from oral teaching or books, yet there do exist books on military affairs written by great men which you should certainly not neglect.[144] A gen-

eral should also understand the power and use of war-machines. You see that your father is extremely resourceful in this respect; I know of no one who has investigated machines with greater zeal or (possibly) built more things of this kind.

Last of all—a matter not unrelated to the foregoing—young 68 men should acquire skill in swimming, a thing which Augustus Caesar was so eager to have his nephews taught (he had no sons) that he often would teach them himself.[145] This skill generally frees people from great dangers and makes them bolder in naval battles and crossing rivers. And in this entire category of matters pertaining to military exercises, you have two older brothers to imitate, Francesco and Giacomo, noblemen widely known for their skill in arms and renowned for their complete prudence and self-control. It is always suitable for you to show them trust, faithfulness and respect, as you do, and to imitate them so correctly that you may yourself set an an example of virtue and provide a bulwark against misfortune for your younger relatives. The fellowship of the human race is strongest when obligations of blood are sacred, and reverence toward superiors, kindness toward inferiors, and moderation and good nature among equals is preserved.

Leisure and Relaxation

But since we cannot always be engaged in work, but must from 69 time to time indulge in relaxation, let us now set out a method and program in this area. The first and most important principle is not to take up any base or harmful sport unless it either sharpens diligence or exercises bodily strength to some extent. Scipio and Laelius, and (now and again) the augur Scaevola, Laelius' son-in-law, used for relaxation to collect pebbles and small shells on the seashores or in riverbeds; this activity became practically a necessity for them, for they used to go collecting only after they had discharged great labors or had arrived at an advanced age. In this regard the practice of the same Scaevola is perhaps more praiseworthy. He is said to have been an excellent ball-player, a recreation he used to take up particularly to restore his powers and strengthen his chest when tired from the law courts and from his labors in interpreting the civil law.[146] A devotion to hunting, fowling, and fishing also falls into this category; such activities refresh the spirit with great delight and the movement and effort they require strengthen the limbs,

with zeal gently deceiving severe labor,[147]

as Horace says. For unless these things were seasoned with great pleasure, who is there who would spontaneously wish to undergo such toil, whose strength could endure them? To be sure, it was this very thing, [toil and endurance], that the laws of Lycurgus aimed at, not the recreation of adolescents. Or if these things perchance seem too onerous to relieve young men tired out by study, let them either be absolutely quiet, or do some gentle riding, or take a pleasant walk; they may even tell jokes and witticisms to one another so long as they are in good taste, a custom the Spartans used for relaxation. The *Life of Lycurgus* describes in detail the usefulness of this custom.[148]

70 Nor will it be unseemly to relax the mind with singing and playing the lute, as we mentioned above. This was the custom of the Pythagoreans,[149] and it was once a celebrated fact among the archaic heroes that Homer depicted Achilles withdrawing from battle and resting this way — singing praises of mighty men, to be sure, not love songs.[150] For leisure we can, then, either do the same thing ourselves or appreciate others who are doing so, adopting those musical modes which seem most suited to us and our times. Sicilian modes are best for rest and relaxation; French modes, on the contrary, excite and motivate; Italian ones keep to the mean between these two.[151] Likewise, music made by singing or percus-

sion is quite seemly; while whistling is less suitable to gentle-men.[152] Dancing to music and group dances with women might seem to be pleasures unworthy of a man. Yet there might be a certain profit in them, since they exercise the body and bring dexterity to the limbs, if they did not make young men lustful and vain, corrupting good behavior.

Not so the game board, since it offers a semblance of fighting and hostile contest; Palamedes, as the oldest authors say, invented the game during the Trojan War in order to occupy his soldiers with this diversion and keep his army, thus distracted, from mutiny.[153] The game of dice on the other hand either fosters a greed unsuited to a free person, or a softness unbefitting a man. Those who play dice for the sake of gain might be better off engaging in more profitable businesses, but those who hunt pleasure here are slow-witted, as they cannot find any more honorable pleasure. Pleasure is most suitably taken in games that require some or even great skill, and as little chance as possible. Although, perhaps, someone might think it acceptable to spend one's leisure on this art, as there exist literary treatments of such matters; or influenced by the greatness of an author, he might think it not unseemly to do what that author has thought it seemly to write about. Claudius Caesar, for instance, published a book on the game of dice,[154] a pursuit usually enjoyed by people who love this one thing only, with the result that they neglect all their property and indeed waste their entire lives. 71

However, for those who take pleasure in literary studies, a variety of reading brings comfort and new readings relieve the boredom of old ones. From time to time, however, one needs to do absolutely nothing and be entirely free from work, so as to meet once again the demands of work and toil. For the muscle which is always stretched taut usually breaks if it is not sometimes relaxed — though for the wise man there is no time more toilsome than when he is doing nothing — assuming the wise man *could* do noth- 72 ing.[155] We have heard that certain people are accustomed to apportion their time as follows: that over a day and a night they allow a third of their time to sleep, a third to recoup their strength and find respite from work, and they give the rest to liberal studies. For my part, I am not ready to condemn this plan, but I cannot entirely commend it, either. This, however, I can affirm and affirm boldly: that the less of our life that slips away from us, and the longer we live on this account, the more of our time we should liberate for good letters.

Grooming the Body

73 Finally, let us now touch on the grooming of the body: how to keep it decently—neither too fastidious nor slovenly[156]—and make it suitable to the business at hand, the place, and the time, but especially to the person. It is not appropriate to sit in school with a crown on ones' head or to take clothing off, or to go into battle in a flowing gown or a long-sleeved tunic, nor should the son of a prince be seen wearing a cheap, dirty tunic like a commoner, or a worn cape. Excessive concern for grooming and attractiveness is the sign of a feminine mind and a proof of great vanity. Nevertheless, young men are entitled to certain indulgences, nor are all their errors to be punished by harsh reproof, for unless they satisfy the demands of youth in some respects, they will carry the vices of that time of life into old age.

74 I have written the foregoing for you, Ubertino, as I promised at the beginning, not to remind you that you should be doing something, but to show you to yourself.[157] If you follow nature's lead, you will have no need of a counsellor to achieve the highest virtue. For unless you should fail yourself, your innate gifts seem to offer brilliant promise in everything that concerns you. But if I seem to

grant you certain titles of praise, I would have you consider them, in accepting them from me, more as a spur for good deeds than as a reward for deeds well done. So it is right for you to strive with all your strength to prove yourself to be a man who worthily corresponds to these noble beginnings of your adolescence. Use well the gifts of nature; do not be false to those outstanding qualities you possess. For my sake, don't allow me to be thought a false prophet or a vain prognosticator in your regard. If you act correctly, you shall have praise from everyone in your time, and you will be commended to posterity in my literary compositions, if I possess any ability of this kind. If you do not, there will be one person — myself — who will dare to say plainly and admit openly that the only thing that failed you was yourself.

LEONARDO BRUNI
THE STUDY OF LITERATURE
TO LADY BATTISTA MALATESTA
OF MONTEFELTRO[1]

I feel myself constrained, dear lady, by many successive reports of   1
your wonderful virtues to write to you in commendation of the
perfect development of those innate powers of which I have heard
so much that is excellent, or, if that is too much, at least to urge
you, through these literary efforts of mine, to bring them to such a
perfection. There is, indeed, no lack of examples of women renowned for literary study and eloquence that I could mention to
exhort you to excellence. Cornelia, the daughter of Scipio, wrote
letters in the most elegant of styles, which letters survived for
many centuries after her death.[2] The poetical works of Sappho
were held in the highest honor among the Greeks for their unique
eloquence and literary skill.[3] Then, too, there was Aspasia, a
learned lady of the time of Socrates, who was outstanding in eloquence and literature, and from whom even so great a philosopher
as Socrates did not blush to admit he had learned certain things.[4]
I could mention still others, but let these three stand sufficient as
examples of the most renowned women. Be encouraged and elevated by their excellence!

It is not fitting that such understanding and intellectual power   2
as you possess were given you in vain, not fitting that you should
be satisfied with mediocrity; such gifts expect and encourage the
highest excellence. And your glory will be all the brighter, for
those other women flourished in ages when there was an abundance of learned persons whose very number decreases the estimation in which we must hold them, while you live in these times
when learning has so far decayed that it is regarded as positively

miraculous to meet a learned man, let alone a woman. By learning, however, I do not mean that confused and vulgar sort such as is possessed by those who nowadays profess theology, but a legitimate and liberal[5] kind which joins literary skill with factual knowledge,[6] a learning Lactantius possessed, and Augustine, and Jerome, all of whom were finished men of letters as well as great theologians. It is shameful, by contrast, how very little modern theologians know of letters.

3　　But I digress. Let me rather pursue our discourse, not for you to be instructed by me (for of that I imagine you have no need), but simply for you to understand my views on the subject of literary study.

4　　The person aiming at the kind of excellence to which I am calling you needs first, I think, to acquire no slender or common, but a wide and exact, even recherché familiarity with literature. Without this basis, no one can build himself any high or splendid thing. The one who lacks knowledge of literature will neither understand sufficiently the writings of the learned, nor will he be able, if he himself attempts to write, to avoid making a laughingstock of himself. To attain this knowledge, elementary instruction has its place, but much more important is our own effort and study. Elementary instruction, indeed, need hardly detain us. Everyone knows that in the first instance the mind needs an instructor to train and as it were initiate it so that it can recognize not only the parts of speech and their arrangement, but also those smaller details and elements of speech. But these we absorb in childhood as though dreaming; afterwards when we have moved on to greater things, they somehow come back to our lips, and it is only then that we taste their sweetness and true flavor. There is another more robust kind of elementary instruction, useful more to adults than children: the instruction, I mean, of those who are called grammarians, those who have thoroughly investigated every detail in our books, and in so doing have created a kind of literary discipline. Servius and Priscian are grammarians of this sort.

But believe me, our own study is far more important. Study reveals and explains to us not only the words and syllables but also the tropes and figures of speech in all their beauty and polish. Through study we receive our literary formation, and, as it were, our teaching; through it, indeed, we learn much that a teacher could never teach us: vocalic melody, elegance, concinnity, and charm. The most important rule of study is to see to it that we study only those works that are written by the best and most approved authors, and avoid the crude and ignorant writings which only ruin and degrade our natural abilities. The reading of clumsy and corrupt writers imbues the reader with their own vices and infests his mind with a similar corruption. Study is, so to speak, the pabulum of the mind by which the intellect is trained and nourished. For this reason, just as gastronomes are careful in the choice of what they put in their stomachs, so those who wish to preserve purity of taste will only allow certain reading to enter their minds. 5

This then will be our first study: to read only the best and most approved authors. Our second will be to bring to this reading a keen critical sense. The reader must study the reasons why the words are placed as they are, and the meaning and force of each element of the sentence, the smaller as well as the larger; he must thoroughly understand the force of the several particles whose idiom and usage he will copy from the authors he reads.[7] 6

Hence a woman who enjoys sacred literature and wishes to avoid unhealthy literature will take up Augustine and Jerome and any authors she finds similar to them, such as Ambrose and Cyprian. But the greatest of all those who have ever written of the Christian religion, the one who excells them all with his brilliance and richness of expression, is Lactantius Firmianus, without doubt the most eloquent of all Christian authors, and the one whose elo- 7 quence and technique are best able to nourish and educate the type of ability I am considering. I recommend most of all his volumes *Against False Religion,* and also *On the Wrath of God,* and *The Creation of Man.* Please do read them if you love literature, and you will be steeped in a pleasure like ambrosia and nectar. If you have any translations of Gregory Nazianzen, John Chrysostom, or St. Basil the Great, the Greek Doctors of the Church, I advise you to read them, too — so long as you read them in good Latin translations, not perversions.[8]

8   A woman, on the other hand, who enjoys secular literature will choose Cicero, a man — Good God! — so eloquent! so rich in expression! so polished! so unique in every kind of excellence! Next will be Vergil, the delight and ornament of our literature, then Livy and Sallust and the other poets and writers in their order will follow close behind. With them she will train and strengthen her taste, and she will be careful, when she is obliged to say or write something, to use no word she has not first met in one of these authors.

9   It will moreover be profitable for her from time to time to make an effort to read well aloud. For in prose, as well as in verse, there are certain rhythms, inflexions, and pacings, an orchestration, as it were, recognized and measured by the sense of hearing, which causes the voice at one moment to drop and at another to rise, and to create beautifully ordered connections between the cola, commata, and periods.[9] This is readily apparent in every good writer. She will clearly grasp this when she reads aloud and she will fill her ears with it as with a harmony, and will hear it also afterwards when she writes, and will imitate it. Another result of her reading will be to have each word drop in place at its proper time, so that there is never haste when there should be emphasis, nor emphasis when haste is called for.

10   Again, I would not have her ignorant of writing. I do not now speak of penmanship (although I commend whoever possesses

that skill), but the formation of letters and syllables. She should understand how each is to be written, the nature of the letters and the movement from one to another, which letters can be combined and which cannot stand next to one another. This is a small matter, of course, but it is a significant mark of our education, which betrays manifest ignorance in those who lack it. She ought also to recite and memorize the quantity of every syllable, that is, whether it is long, short, or common. This knowledge is necessary to understand many passages which would otherwise be unintelligible, such as that of Vergil,

> Each with his hair bound by a trimmed garland in the
> traditional manner[10]

and a thousand other examples. It is likewise most unseemly for one who fancies oneself a *littérateur* to misunderstand so basic a thing as the quantity of syllables, especially since verse is universally held to be no contemptible part of literature, but verses are made up of feet, and feet are constituted by the quantity of their syllables. What promise there is for someone who does not understand quantity, what poetical taste he can possibly have, is something I do not for my part clearly understand.

This knowledge is likewise necessary, I believe, in composing and writing prose.[11] Meter is not absent from prose simply because the multitude do not perceive it; it is in fact the source of aural sweetness and pleasure. It makes a great difference, according to Aristotle, which meters are used at the beginning and end of a sentence, and even in the middle there are certain meters which are preferable and others which should be avoided. He himself particularly approves of the paean, which has two forms: a long followed by three short beats, or three shorts followed by a long. He considers the latter suitable for *clausulae*, and the former for the beginnings of sentences and perfectly appropriate in the middle as well. He disapproves of the dactyl and the iamb in the middle: the

11

former he considers too elevated, and the latter too low.[12] Cicero's favorite meters in *clausulae* are the dichoreus, which is made up of two trochees, the cretic, which is long-short-long, and the aforementioned paean. He holds the iamb to be the most appropriate in the middle of the period when we are employing a low or ordinary style, and when a fuller style is being employed, the dactyl, the paean, or the dochimius (a five-syllable foot: a short, two long, a short, and a long), which latter rhythm he considers to be suitable in all parts of the sentence.[13] Moreover, it is clear that argument, narration, and lamentation all have their several rhythms appropriate to them. Anger and mental excitation do not accept the spondee, requiring as they do a quick and hasty rhythm; narration and instruction, on the contrary, demand deliberate and stable rhythms, and so are averse to "headlong" feet. Thus, every variety of communication has its appropriate rhythm. Any writer who ignores this fact would be writing as chance directs, like a man stumbling in the dark.

12   There will, perhaps, be many who think exaggerated my attention to this point. They must remember, however, that I am speaking of persons of great abilities and promise. Mediocrities may go, or rather crawl, as they can. It is sure that no one will reach the pinnacle of literary skill except by knowledge of and practice in all these things. Then, too, the purpose of my treatise is to cover the whole field of literature: not only normal practice, but also the glories, the elegancies, and the finer charms of discourse. I would have our writer possess a rhetorical *garniture de toilette*, a fine wardrobe, an abundant stock of domestic furniture, if I may call it that, which she can produce and display as the need arises for every type of writing.

13   Having said that genuine learning was a combination of literary skill and factual knowledge, we have set forth our view of what literary skill is. Let us now, therefore, say something about knowledge. Here again I prefer that someone whose intellect shows the

greatest promise possess the most ardent desire for learning. Let her despise no branch of learning, hold all the world as her province, and, in a word, burn marvellously with a desire for knowledge and understanding. An ardent and well-motivated person like this needs, I think, to be applauded and spurred on in some directions, while in others she must be reined in and called back. Disciplines there are, which it is not fitting to ignore completely, yet it is by no means glorious to completely master. In geometry and arithmetic, for example, if she should waste a great deal of time worrying about their subtle obscurities, I would seize her and tear her away from them. I would do the same in astrology, and even, perhaps, in the art of rhetoric.

I make this last point with some hesitation, since if any living 14 men have labored in this art, I profess myself to be of their number. But there are many things here to be taken into account, the first of which is the person whom I am addressing. For why should the subtleties of the *status*, the *epicheiremata*, the *krinomena*,[14] and a thousand other rhetorical conundrums consume the powers of a woman, who will never see the forum? That art of delivery, which the Greeks call *hypocrisis* and we *pronunciatio*, and which Demosthenes said was the first, the second, and the third most important acquirement of the orator,[15] so far is that from being the concern of a woman that if she should gesture energetically with her arms as she spoke and shout with violent emphasis, she would probably be thought mad and put under restraint. The contests of the forum, like those of warfare and battle, are the sphere of men. Hers will not be the task of learning to speak for and against witnesses, for and against torture, for and against reputation; she will not practice the commonplaces, or think about the sly anticipation of an opponent's arguments. She will, in a word, leave the rough-and-tumble of the forum entirely to men.

When, then, will I encourage her, when will I spur her on? Just 15 when she devotes herself to divinity and moral philosophy. It is there I will beg her to spread her wings, there apply her mind, there spend her vigils. It will be worth our while to dwell on this in some detail. First, let the Christian woman yearn to acquire a knowledge of sacred letters. What better advice could I give? Let her search much, weigh much, examine much in this branch of study. But let her fondness be for the older authors. The moderns, if they are good men, let her honor and revere, but she should pay scant attention to their writings. A woman of literature will find no instruction in them that is not in St. Augustine, and St. Augustine, moreover, unlike them, has the diction of an educated person, and one well worth attending to.

16   Nor would I have her rest content with a knowledge of sacred literature; let her broaden her interests into secular studies as well. Let her know what the most excellent minds among the philosophers have taught about moral philosophy, what their doctrines are concerning continence, temperance, modesty, justice, courage, and liberality. She should understand their beliefs about happiness: whether virtue is in itself sufficient for happiness, or whether torture, poverty, exile, or prison can impede our progress toward it. Whether, when such misfortunes befall the blessed, they are made miserable thereby, or whether they simply take away happiness without inducing actual misery. Whether human felicity consists in pleasure and the absence of pain, as Epicurus would have it, or in moral worth, as Zeno believed, or in the exercise of virtue, which was Aristotle's view.[16] Believe me, such subjects as these are beautiful and intellectually rewarding. They are valuable not only for the guidance they give in life, but they also supply us with a certain marvellous variety of expressions for every kind of writing and speaking.

17   These two subjects, then, divinity and moral philosophy, will be her most important goals, the *raisons d'être* of her studies. Other subjects will be related to them in proportion as they contribute to them or to their embellishment. It is true that the marvel of hu-

man excellence, that excellence which raises a name to genuine celebrity, is a direct result of a wide and various knowledge; and it is true, too, that we should read much and learn much, selecting, acquiring, weighing, and examining all things from all points of view, from which process we derive great benefit for our studies. Yet at the same time we should choose carefully and consider thoughtfully the time at our disposal in order to give preference to those things that are most important and most useful.[17]

To the aforesaid subjects there should first be joined, in my view, a knowledge of history, which is a subject no scholar should neglect. It is a fit and seemly thing to be familiar with the origins and progress of one's own nation, and with the deeds in peace and in war of great kings and free peoples. Knowledge of the past gives guidance to our counsels and our practical judgment, and the consequences of similar undertakings [in the past] encourages or deters us according to our circumstances in the present. History, moreover, will be the most commodious source of that stock of examples of outstanding conduct with which it is fitting frequently to embellish our conversation. Then, too, some of the outstanding historians are distinguished and polished writers as well, and so make valuable reading for literary purposes: Livy, I mean, and Sallust and Tacitus and Curtius, and especially Julius Caesar, who described his own deeds with the greatest ease and elegance in his *Commentaries*. These, then, the woman of high promise will go on to acquire, the more so as they make pleasant reading. For here there are no subtleties to be unravelled, no knotty *quaestiones* to be untied, for history consists entirely of narrations of facts that are easy to grasp, and, once grasped (at least by an outstanding mind such as I am considering), will never be forgotten.

I will further urge her not to neglect the orators. Where else is virtue praised with such passion and vice condemned with such ferocity? It is the orators who will teach us to praise the good deed and to hate the bad; it is they who will teach us how to soothe, en-

18

19

courage, stimulate, or deter. All these things the philosophers do, it is true, but in some special way anger, mercy, and the arousal and pacification of the mind are completely within the power of the orator. Then, too, those figures of speech and thought, which like stars or torches illuminate our diction and give it distinction, are the proper tools of the orator which we will borrow from them when we speak or write, and turn to our use as the occasion demands. In sum, all the richness, power, and polish in our expression, its lifeblood, as it were, we will derive from the orators.

20   The poets, too, I would have her read and understand. This is a knowledge which all great men have possessed. Aristotle, at least, frequently cites passages of Homer, Hesiod, Pindar, Euripides, and the other poets, showing by his familiar knowledge and ready quotation of them that he was no less a student of the poets than of the philosophers. Plato as well makes frequent use of the poets, bringing them in freely, even gratuitously; indeed, he often uses their authority to confirm his own. So much for the Greeks; what of the Latin writers? Is Cicero to be thought too little versed in poetical knowledge when, not content with Ennius, Pacuvius, Accius, and the other Latin poets, he fills his works with his own renderings from the Greek poets? What of the stern and austere Seneca: did not even he write poems, and does he not completely gush forth in verse now and again? I pass over Augustine, Jerome, Lactantius and Boethius, whose writings show a great knowledge of poetry.

21   In my view, the man who has not read the poets is, as it were, maimed as regards literature. The poets have many wise and useful things to say about life and how it should be lived; in them are to be found the origins and causes of nature and birth—the seeds, as it were, of all teachings. By their antiquity and their reputation for wisdom they possess a high authority, by their elegance they have acquired a splendor and a distinction, by their nobility they have so far made themselves a worthy study for free men, that

whoever does not know them seems to be something of a rustic. Does Homer lack any sort of wisdom that we should refuse him the repute of being most wise? Some say that his poetry provides a complete doctrine of life, divided into periods of peace and war. And indeed in the affairs of war, what has he not told us of the prudence of the general, of the cunning and bravery of the soldier, of the kinds of trickery to be allowed or omitted, of advice, of counsel? Aeneas, being in a certain battle the leader of the Trojans, has driven the Greeks with great force of arms back to their lines, and is recklessly urging his men on, when, just as he is about to throw his entire force against the Greeks, Hector speeds to him and advises him to act with caution and prudence, saying that a man who leads an army needs caution more than reckless bravery. How valuable a precept, by the immortal God, especially coming from the brave Hector![18] Nowadays our generals, ignoring this counsel and using rashness instead of caution, have brought great ruin and wretched slaughter upon themselves and their men. In the same author, we see Iris, having been sent to Agamemnon and finding him asleep, rouse him and reprove him for sleeping when so great a responsibility is his and the safety of his people has been committed to his care.[19] Here again, how wise this is! — whether you want to call it a teaching or a counsel or an admonition. Did Socrates or Plato or Pythagoras ever give better or holier advice to a general? And he has ten thousand more such counsels which I would gladly speak of, did I not fear being too prolix. And again in the affairs of peace his precepts are as many and as excellent.

But come, lest we attribute all to Homer and the Greeks, let us consider the great value of our Vergil's wisdom when he reveals, as from an oracle or from the secret places of nature: 22

> Know first, the heav'ns, and earth's broad glist'ning fields,
> fair Cynthia's seat, and far, the starry seas,
> an inward spirit feeds; and through each joint,

throughout the shapeless mass infused, doth stir
a Mind that mingles with the mighty whole.
Thence man- and cattle-kind, thence soar th'aerial
beasts, and thence from 'neath the flashing waves
doth Ocean's shudd'ring prodigies come forth.
Fire throughout each vein doth lively surge
and every seed tells of its heav'nly birth.[20]

And so on. Can we esteem the philosophers at such a rate when
we read passages such as this? Which of them ever laid bare the
nature and essence of soul with such knowledge? What about
when the same poet, as though divinely inspired, prophesied just
before Our Lord's birth in these words:

Now comes the earth's last age, now in full Time
springs th'order new: thus spake the Cumaean rhyme.
Now comes the Virgin, now Saturnian states
return anew, and now from Heaven's gate
comes down Heav'n's offspring, Earth's renewèd race.[21]

The wisest of the ancients tell us that the divine mind dwells in
the poets, and that they are called *vates*[22] because they speak not so
much of their own accord as through a divine inspiration, in a
kind of higher mental state. Though here Vergil appeals to the
authority of the Cumaean Sibyl, who, as Lactantius shows, had
predicted the advent of Christ.[23] The Sibyl then did prophesy
Christ's coming, but did not clearly reveal the time when He
would come; but Vergil, born many ages after the Sibyl, recognized that that time was now come and announced in wonder and
amazement "the new offspring sent from Heaven."

23   And still some say we should not read the poets, that we should
never taste a branch of literature that I might with exact truth
pronounce divine! Such persons are most often those who, having
no training in polite learning themselves, in consequence neither

understand nor value in literature any excellent thing. My view of the matter is that poetical knowledge is of primary importance in our education, alike for its utility, as aforesaid — that wide and various acquaintance we get with facts — and for the brilliance of its language. Moreover, it is the *quickest* of our studies: we learn it while young when we can concentrate on practically nothing else; its rounded rhythms make it easy to retain; it accompanies us everywhere, and comes back to us spontaneously without need for books, so that you may study it even when doing something else.

And the degree to which poetry accords with nature may, I 24 think, be seen from the fact that common, uneducated persons without any knowledge of letters or learning, if they have the wit, enjoy the employment of their crude powers in making certain sounds and rhythms. Even when their sense would be better and more easily expressed in prose, they think they have made something worth hearing only when they have stuck it into verse. Again, when Mass is being said in church, we sometimes yawn and fall asleep even when it is being done very beautifully, but when once that poetical refrain breaks out, the *Primo dierum omnium,* or the *Iste Confessor,* or the *Ut queant laxis resonare fibris,* which of us is so earthbound as not to feel some lifting up of the soul, some inspired feeling? It is for this reason that certain of the ancients believed the soul to be a number and a harmony.[24] It was certain (they thought) that all things in accordance with nature enjoyed that which was most similar and related to themselves, and there was nothing which so softened and delighted our souls as harmony and number. But this is another and greater subject. For the moment, this only do I wish to be understood: that it is to poetry, more than to any other branch of letters, that nature attracts us; that it possesses a great deal of utility, pleasure, and nobility; and that that man who has no knowledge of it can by no means be said to be liberally educated.

25   I have, I realize, gone on about poetry rather more than I had at first intended; once started, it is more difficult to control the multitude of ideas that seem to come thronging around of their own accord than to find what it is one should be saying. But I was the more inclined to do so as I am aware that a prince of your house,[25] if he should happen to hear of this discourse of mine, will object to this part of it. He is, to be sure, a man born for high deeds and outstanding for the number and greatness of his virtues, but a stubborn fellow in debate, who is reluctant to abandon a position once taken. So having sometime declared that we should not read the poets, he will pursue his error even unto death. But I want no quarrel with him, especially in writing, for even in his absence I owe him the deepest reverence.

26   But I should be perfectly willing to ask of a certain other person among those who attack the poets why it is we should not read them. Having no clear case against them, he will charge the poets with containing tales of love affairs and sexual misconduct. But I would dare affirm that in no other writers can be found so many examples of womanly modesty and goodness: Penelope's chastity and faithfulness to Ulysses,[26] Alcestis' wonderful modesty towards Admetus,[27] the marvelous constancy of both in the face of calamities and long separation from their husbands. Many such instances can be read in the poets, the finest patterns of the wifely arts. Yes; *amours* are sometimes described, such as the tale of Phoebus and Daphne,[28] and of Vulcan and Venus,[29] but who is so doltish as not to understand that such things are fictional and allegorical? The things to be condemned, moreover, are very few, while many are the things that are good and well worth the knowing, as I showed above with Homer and Vergil. It is the height of injustice to forget about the things that truly deserve praise, and to remember only those things that suit one's own argument. "I would be pure," says my austere critic; "I would rather abandon the good in fear of the evil than run the risk of evil in hope of

something good; hence I may neither read the poets myself nor allow others to do so." But Plato and Aristotle studied them, and I will refuse to allow that they yield to you either in moral seriousness or in practical understanding. Or do you think you see farther than they?

"I am a Christian," my critic says. But are you suggesting that they lived without morality? As though honor and moral seriousness were something different then from what they are now! As though the same and even worse cannot be found in the Holy Scriptures! Do we not find there depicted Samson's wild lusts, when he put his mighty head in a wench's lap and was shorn of his strength-giving hair?[30] Is this not poetical? And is this not shameful? I pass over in silence the shocking crime of Lot's daughters,[31] the detestable filthiness of the Sodomites,[32] two circumstances that I, praiser of poets though I be, can hardly bear to relate. Why even mention David's passion for Bathsheba, his crime against Uriah,[33] Solomon's fratricide[34] and his flock of concubines?[35] All of these stories are wicked, obscene, and disgusting, yet shall we say that the Bible is not therefore to be read? Surely not. Then neither are the poets to be rejected because of the occasional reference to human pleasures. For my part, whenever I read Vergil's account of the affair of Dido and Aeneas,[36] I am so lost in admiration of his poetical genius that I scarcely attend to the thing itself, knowing it to be a fiction. Other poetical fictions affect me the same way. My concupiscence is not aroused, since I know the circumstances to be fictional and allegorical in intent. When I read the Scriptures, on the contrary, knowing the facts to be true, I suffer temptation.

But I don't insist; I am perfectly willing to abandon a little of my ground, especially given that I am addressing a woman. I admit that, just as there are distinctions between nobles and commoners, so too among the poets there are certain grades of respectability. If somewhere a comic poet has made his theme too

27

28

explicit, if a satirist excoriates vice a little too frankly, let her avert her gaze and not read them. For these are the plebian poets. The aristocrats of poesy, Vergil, I mean, and Seneca and Statius and the others of their sort, must be read if she is not to do without the greatest ornaments of literature. And without them, she may not hope for glory.

29   In sum, then, the excellence of which I speak comes only from a wide and various knowledge. It is necessary to read and comprehend a great deal, and to bestow great pains on the philosophers, the poets, the orators and historians and all the other writers. For thus comes that full and sufficient knowledge we need to appear eloquent, well-rounded, refined, and widely cultivated. Needed too is a well-developed and respectable literary skill of our own. For the two together reinforce each other and are mutually beneficial. Literary skill without knowledge is useless and sterile; and knowledge, however extensive, fades into the shadows without the glorious lamp of literature.[37] Of what advantage is it to know many fine things if one has neither the ability to talk of them with distinction or write of them with praise? And so, literary skill and factual knowledge are in a manner of speaking wedded to each other. It was the two joined together that advanced the glory and fame of those ancients whose memory we venerate: Plato, Democritus, Aristotle, Theophrastus, Varro, Cicero, Seneca, Augustine, Jerome, Lactantius, with all of whom we can scarce decide whether it is their knowledge or their literary power that is the greater.

30   To conclude: the intellect that aspires to the best, I maintain, must be in this way doubly educated, and it is for the sake of acquiring these two knowledges that we mass up our reading; yet we must also take stock of the time at our disposal, devoting ourselves only to the most important and the most useful subjects, and not waste time with the obscure and profitless. It is religion and moral philosophy that ought to be our particular studies, I think, and

the rest studied in relation to them as their handmaids, in proportion as they aid or illustrate their meaning; and it is with this in mind that we must fix upon the poets, orators, and other writers. In literary study care should be taken to employ noble precepts and long and perceptive observation, and never to read any but the best and most approved books.

Such are my opinions about the study of literature, although if 31 you hold different views, I shall willingly yield to you. For I have not written to you as master to pupil (I should not presume so much), but simply as one of the crowd of your admirers, who want to unite my convictions with yours and, as they say, cheer the runner on to victory. Farewell.

AENEAS SILVIUS PICCOLOMINI
THE EDUCATION OF BOYS

To his lord, the most serene prince, Ladislas, king of Hungary and   1
Bohemia and duke of mighty Austria, Aeneas, bishop of Trieste,
sends hearty greetings.

If there is anyone who ought to devote himself to virtue and to   2
dedicate himself entirely to good deeds, no reasonable man will
deny that that person is you, illustrious King Ladislas. For after
you have completed the years of your tutelage, you will be expected to rule great kingdoms and extensive realms, and you will
be unable to govern long unless you become a man of consummate
prudence. Kingdoms are obedient to virtue; they resist vice. As
formerly Rome did not tolerate cowardice in an emperor, so now
Hungary despises sloth in a king. No one needs wisdom more
than a sovereign; and how shall a man undone by his own errors
govern others rightly?[1] A foolish king destroys both himself and
his people;[2] for a wise king all things turn out for the best.
"Through me," says Wisdom, "kings reign, and lawgivers discern
what is just."[3] Allow yourself to be imbued with the best precepts,
therefore, while you are a boy, and as you grow to manhood.

You should also be incited to these ideals by the example of   3
your forbears, both paternal and maternal, who ruled the Roman
empire in the most praiseworthy fashion, as well as by the example
of your father Albert, of honored and imperishable memory. It
would be most shameful for you to be an unworthy descendent of
such as these. It is fitting that he who inherits the realms of his
forbears should also inherit their virtues. You are succeeding to
men of noble rank: take care that you become likewise their heir
in virtue. Nobility clothed in holy morals is deserving of praise.

Nothing vicious is noble. For who would call a man noble who is unworthy of his family and distinguished only by a famous name?[4] Indeed, as no one considers mute animals of superior stock unless they are brave, even when sprung of excellent sires,[5] so men cannot rightly be called noble unless they are commended by their own virtue. It is a poor thing, as Juvenal says,

> to lean upon the fame of others,
> lest the pillars give way, and the house fall in ruins.[6]

4   The pursuit of learning, moreover, offers the greatest assistance in acquiring virtue, and this learning becomes no one better than a king. Knowing this, a Roman emperor in a letter strongly exhorted the king of the Franks, with whom he was then allied in friendship, to take care that his children be instructed in learning, saying that an illiterate king was like a crowned ass. Nor, as I have discovered, were the Roman emperors uneducated, so long as the commonwealth flourished. At home and abroad, in the senate and in the army, learning ruled; but it is evident to everybody that all the virtues languished once letters were neglected. For both military strength and the imperial power itself were weakened as though cut off from their root.[7] Indeed, Boethius relates that Socrates thought commonwealths were fortunate if their rulers happened to be lovers of wisdom.[8] For those men alone are perfect who strive to mingle political roles with philosophy and who procure for themselves a double good: their lives are devoted to the general benefit, and, exposed to no disturbances, are spent with the greatest tranquillity in the pursuit of philosophy. Therefore princes and all who are destined to rule must endeavor with all their strength to take part in public life and to lay hold of philosophy in so far as it will seem appropriate for the times. Thus did Pericles conduct his public duties, likewise Architas of Tarentum, Dion of Syracuse, and the Theban Epaminondas, two of whom, according to Plutarch, are known to have been disciples of Plato.[9]

I pass over our Scipios, Fabiuses, Catos, Marcelluses, and Caesars, all of whom attained high renown and deep learning. We therefore wish that, when the time comes, you will rule after their fashion, so that under your leadership Hungary, wearied by great disasters, and Bohemia, crushed by the cruel errors of heresy, may breathe once more and be restored to their ancient splendor. We shall obtain this undoubtedly if future events fulfill the promise you hold out. For we have drawn from you a pleasant odor "like the fragrance of a full field which the Lord has blessed."[10] It is a great mark of future righteousness that you are unable to see or hear shameful deeds. You do not approve of immoral companions; you listen with the closest attention to tales of virtue, and day by day you strive to become better through the instruction of your teacher.

Your instructor, Kaspar, who honors and loves you very much, 5 has spoken to me about you in these terms. He is a man as learned as he is upright, at whose entreaty we have undertaken to write this little book for you.[11] He begged us most earnestly to write something suitable and succinct for your instruction and training. We might have wished that this task had been entrusted to someone who could instruct you more elegantly and better than we. Ordinary things are not suited to someone like you, and we ourselves are not the sort who can offer lofty things. But we could not refuse our obligation to obey you nor disregard the wish of your teacher, lest we seem adverse to Your Majesty or an obstacle to your teacher's affection, especially since we are now celebrating the birth of our most loving Savior, at which time it is customary for faithful Christians to exchange gifts. Indeed something should have been given to you at this time, but what can our poverty bestow upon you? We cannot say with the Fisherman "arise and walk," for we are not of such merit, nor, thanks be to God, do you need such assistance. "But gold and silver have I none,"[12] we can try and say; what else can we bestow than that which the prayers of your teacher sought? The precepts of virtue surpass gold and silver;[13] if anyone should prefer horses, garments, or precious stones to these precepts, he is more like a horse or a stone than a wise man. Accordingly, I had planned for Your Majesty a short work which we would give you as a gift on the birthday of Our Lord at the annual pageant of the Church. Somehow the work has increased in our hands: fleeing obscurity, we left behind brevity. As it is, the size of the work makes it neither self-indulgently long nor obscurely brief. Kindly receive and think well of a small gift from a poor home; you will find it small in price but not in value. We shall point out to Your Highness in this book, which we have divided into four parts, what should be the studies of a king as a boy, as a youth, as a grown man, and as one in his declining years, as we have learned this from famous authors. For we hope that you will not only enter upon but also pass out of all these periods of life; and in order to manage them well and happily, you should imbibe whatever is lacking in these pages of ours — and this will not be slight — from other sources. Farewell.

6   All boys who are led to the summit of virtue must have a good disposition and a capacity for learning. But to furnish this is not in your power nor in that of human endeavor; it is a gift of God alone and a celestial good. Few, however, are found who by nature are unteachable. For Quintilian says that as birds are born to fly, horses to run, and beasts to be ferocious, so mental activity and cleverness are peculiar to man, while stupid and intractable persons are no less unnatural than deformed and remarkable bodies in monsters. And although one person excels another in talent, there is no one who cannot achieve something through effort.[14] But we understand that your natural constitution is sound and teachable; it remains, therefore, for you to receive instruction and practice. For as nature is blind without instruction, so instruction is defective without nature. There will be but little advantage in

each, if you take away practice, but perfection may be obtained from these three things together.[15] Apply yourself therefore, with God's help, and after you have received the rules of instruction, embrace the practice of virtue.

In boys there are two things that require instruction: the body 7 and the mind. We shall speak first of the care of the body. For we say, to be sure, that the foetus is formed in the womb of its mother before the soul is infused into it.[16] Next we shall embrace the instruction of the mind. Sometimes we shall treat them together. Some affirm that both should be done together from infancy, that the education of a boy should begin from the first "little fingernail,"[17] as they say. But as this period has passed for you, I hope not unfruitfully, we must hasten on [to the education appropriate to] your time of life. We have you while you are still a boy: listen to the precepts which we give for a boy.

While I am addressing and advising you, I am also addressing 8 and advising all the teachers who have you in their care. They ought to remember what Plutarch writes to the emperor Trajan, stating publicly that faults of pupils redound upon their teachers, and indeed there were a good number of people who ascribed to Seneca the depraved character of Nero. When Socrates had seen a boy of good natural disposition who was ignorant, he is said to have struck his tutor.[18] It is related by the Babylonian Diogenes that Leonidas, the teacher of Alexander, tainted him with certain vices which dogged the mature and soon mighty king from the time of his boyhood education.[19] They are therefore foolish and entirely mad who entrust the care of their sons to anyone at random and without any selection.

I should wish teachers either to be learned (the better situation) 9 or to know that they are not learned. For nothing is worse than those who, having gone a little beyond their first elements, to use the words of Quintilian, "clothe themselves with the false conviction of their own learning."[20] Rightly therefore did Philip of Macedon cause the first elements of learning to be transmitted to his son Alexander by Aristotle, the greatest philosopher of that age.[21] (I know not through what error Leonidas was given his post.) Rightly also did Peleus place Phoenix in charge of Achilles, that he might be for him a leader and a teacher both in speaking and acting. The lives of teachers should be faultless and their morals irreproachable: this is the best proof[22] that they neither have nor tolerate vices. Let them be neither stern and austere nor free and easy; they should be the sort of person you can neither hate nor blame with justice, who speaks often of what is honorable,[23] so that you do not learn from them vices which afterwards must be unlearned. It is very hard to get rid of such vices, for the task of "unteaching" is more burdensome than that of teaching. For this reason they say that Timotheus, who was famous for his skill with the flute, used to demand from those whom another had instructed a fee double that which he received from uninstructed pupils.[24] Certainly the choice has been splendidly made for you, who have such excellent teachers; if you observe their precepts, you can acquire the reputation for being an excellent man and a distinguished king.

10   Just as farmers place fences around their young trees, so it is the duty of your instructors to encircle you with teachings in keeping with a praiseworthy life and with admonitions from which the shoots of the most correct morals will germinate, for to receive a proper education is the source and root of virtue.[25] Yet let them guide you by their advice, not by blows. Although it is customary for pupils to be flogged, and Chrysippus does not disapprove,[26] and the words of Juvenal may be alleged

> fearing the rod, Achilles, already grown to manhood,
> would sing in his native mountains,[27]

yet Quintilian and Plutarch have more weight with me when they say that boys must be led to honorable practices, not by wounds or blows but by admonitions and explanations. Blows are suitable for slaves, not free men. For noble and especially for royal boys, the praise and blame of their elders are more serviceable than their blows. The former incites them to virtuous deeds, the latter restrains them from disgraceful behavior; yet in each case, measure must be applied lest there be excess. For boys honored with unmeasured praise become arrogant, but visited with too much criticism they become broken and low-spirited.[28] Indeed from blows arises a hatred which endures even to manhood, yet nothing is worse for a pupil than to hate his teachers. If you wish to act rightly, you should love them not less than your studies themselves, and you will consider them as the parents, not of your body, but of your mind. This devoted affection is a great aid to study.[29] Listen again to Juvenal:

> May the gods grant that the earth may rest softly upon the
>   shades of our ancestors
> and may fragrant saffrons and perpetual spring bloom over the
>   ashes
> of those who deemed that a teacher should hold the place of a
>   revered parent.[30]

But enough has been said concerning teachers. Let us now 11 consider how teachers should care for your physical development. Whatever habits a child's body forms it wants to preserve subsequently.[31] Therefore you must be careful not to nurture it too delicately or allow it more sleep or rest than it needs. That soft upbringing which we call "indulgence" shatters every nerve of mind and body.[32] You should avoid soft feathers, don't wear silk close to the skin, and dress sometimes in coarse linen. That is the way to make the limbs tougher and more able to endure labor.

And since you are naturally handsome, a progeny worthy of the 12 sceptre, you must strive that your gestures correspond to your appearance: that your expression is regular, that you do not twist your lips[33] nor suck on your tongue nor acquire the vice of drunkenness. Do not imitate the insolence of the servile; don't throw your head back or keep your eyes on the ground; don't bend your neck to either side; don't spread your hands like a rustic, stand in an unbecoming way, or sit in ridiculous postures. The motions of your eyelids must be properly restrained; your arms should be straight, your gait firm and sure. Nothing unbecoming can be pleasing.[34] Philip [of Macedon], the father of Alexander, knew this. Once, when selling [into slavery] a number of men he had captured in war, he laid aside his cumbersome tunic and was sitting in an indecorous attitude. One of those being sold shouted out: "Spare me, Philip; I claim friendship with you through my father." Asked about the source of this friendship, the man drew closer and said in a low voice, "Pull your cloak down a little; you look silly sitting that way." Philip said, "Release him, I overlooked this person who was my friend and well-wisher."[35] So decorum must be observed in every movement and posture. In this matter the Greeks were so painstaking that they composed a set of rules governing gesture which they called *cheironomia*. Socrates approved this, Plato included it among his civil virtues, and Chrysippus did not omit it in his precepts concerning the education of children.[36]

13   There are also certain bodily contests which by no means should be despised, but your instructors in these matters must be obeyed, and you should exert as much effort in them as will be necessary to acquire strong and well-knit limbs. For sturdiness of body in childhood is the foundation of a vigorous old age. And since a king must frequently engage in battle, it is fitting to train in military contests the boy whom the helm of state awaits. War rejects a mere semblance of physical fitness. A lean soldier accustomed to military exercises repels ferocious fighters[37] and columns drawn up for battle. Hence it is appropriate for you, who will often have to fight against the Turks, to practice during your boyhood bending the bow, aiming the arrow, whirling the sling, hurl-

ing the spear, mounting horses,[38] running, jumping, taking part in the chase, and learning to swim. There is no shame in learning any honorable activity. Hear what Vergil relates about the boys of Italy:

First we bring our sons to the rivers
and harden them with harsh cold water;
as boys they stand watch in the hunt and weary the forests;
it is their sport to check the horses and to guide the dart with
the bow.[39]

And I should not forbid boys games, so long as they are not 14 lewd or indecent. I approve of and praise your playing ball with boys your own age, in accordance with the rules that the learned Johann Hinderbach[40] composed for you. There is the hoop; there are other perfectly respectable boyish games, which your teachers should sometimes allow you for the sake of relaxation and to stimulate a lively disposition. One should not always be intent on schooling and serious affairs, nor should huge tasks be imposed upon boys, for they may be crushed with exhaustion by such labors, and in any case if they feel overcome by irksome burdens they may be less receptive to learning. For plants which are drowned by too much watering may be nourished by a moderate supply. We should recognize that our life is divided into two parts: study and relaxation. As sleep goes with wakefulness, peace with war, summer with winter, and workdays with feastdays, so rest is the seasoning of labor.[41] Thus one should not take on excessive labor nor indulge in rest beyond measure. For the enemies of instruction, as Plato says, are labor and sleep.[42]

You now understand the sort of physical training and recre- 15 ations that boys who expect to rule should engage in. Let us now discuss food and drink. Moderate and balanced food, as Jerome writes to Rusticus, is healthy for body and soul.[43] A plan should therefore be put in place so that you take such kinds and such amounts of food as will not burden your body nor encumber the liberty of your soul. And although food which is difficult to digest should be refused,[44] care must nevertheless be taken that you do not eventually come to refuse common foods because you are used to delicate fare. You will not always live in cities; sometimes you will be in camps, in forests, in desert places, where it will be necessary to take coarser food. The boy must be so nourished that when the occasion demands it, he does not shrink from red meat. Moreover, it is fitting to offer a future warrior such food as may produce a strong, not a delicate body. Besides, if someone always eats thrushes, almonds, sugar confections, small birds, domestic kids, and lighter courses, with what dishes shall he then be relieved and cured if he should fall sick?

16   I shall now touch on something which many of your subjects will not like. For what Austrian, Hungarian, or Bohemian gladly listens to discussions about frugality at the table? What in these regions is more trumpeted than culinary luxury and the glory of sumptuous dining? What does more to win praise and approval from his household than the numerous dishes of a rich man's dinner? "He's magnificent," they say, "he's fabulous; I'd serve him with pleasure—a man whose kitchen is always smoking, always sumptuous, who doesn't choke on high prices, who dines in splendor and enjoys rare dishes sought from far and wide, whose cellars are overflowing and open to all." Thus actors, parasites, and knaves are accustomed to speak, those whose sole care in life is their gullet,[45] and who, imitating the gluttony of Sardanapallus, would rather have the neck of a crane than that of a sow. But there is nothing, my fine young man, that a wise man may more fittingly flee than the life of ostentation and following the winds of popular opinion, for in either case he will not have true reason as a guide for living.[46]

17   Useless gossip should be condemned, flatterers shunned. The praise that flows from an infamous mouth is not to be desired.

Your illustrious cousin, emperor Frederick, who now holds the imperial monarchy, shows himself to be as temperate as he is wise; he does not satiate himself with wine or food; he makes do with frugal breakfasts and dinners more frugal still; he does not care what drinkers say of him; he seeks renown from the wise, not from drunkards. But (lest we digress) what is the point of such a large number of dishes, which hold banqueters captive by the diversity of meats and the pleasures of taste? Are not diseases brought on by overindulgence? How many are there who, after they have enjoyed to the full the pleasures of the gullet, are compelled to endure the distress of vomiting, so that what they have shamelessly ingested, they may more shamelessly expel?[47] Your servants, then, will make it known, once they know that you do not have many banquets. I shall not fix a number; let those who guide you take into account issues of health, virtue, kingly dignity, time, and place. Julius Caesar willed that the imperial household should be content with three dishes[48] unless there was a formal banquet. Augustus Caesar at the very height of his power was content with ordinary bread and a few common fish.[49] Someone will say: What about Nero? What about Caligula? What about Vitellius? Did they not attend banquets to excess?[50] Of course; but it is seemly to imitate the best, not the worst; the renowned, not those who have failed to win praise.

Again, it may be added, the table should be regulated one way 18 in Italy, where the heat kills hunger, but otherwise in Germany, where the cold arouses the appetite. We do not deny this. We do not forbid a man with a burning hunger to eat large quantities of food, but we do forbid him to take a great variety of costly foods. We would have you remember the word *convivere* while you are dining: our ancestors would not have said, with the Greeks, *compotationes* ("drinking together") and *commessationes* ("eating together"), as if they came together for the sake of the food and wine, but *convivia*, as if for living together.[51] Socrates said that many people wanted to live in order to eat and drink, but he wanted to eat and drink in order to live.[52] Whoever puts limits on himself to any degree will surely not have expensive dinners; nature is satisfied with few things and small amounts. When Aristotle, that very famous and distinguished man, used to discuss the pleasures of taste and touch, that is, of food and love, he would assert that the pleasures arising from these senses were the only ones common to men and beasts, and that therefore anyone devoted to these pleasures should be classed with cattle and wild animals. "The remaining pleasures arising from the other three senses are proper only to man,"[53] as Eustathius declares in Macrobius's *Saturnalia*: "What person, then, with any human decency would be gladdened by these two pleasures of lust and eating, which are common to the ass and the sow?"[54] But concerning the pleasures of love it will be necessary to warn the young man more than the boy. Meanwhile, as we are censuring expensive dinners, Cato the Elder comes to mind, who when he was inveighing against prodigality and excessive expenses among the Roman people said, "Bah! how hard it is to converse with the stomach, which has no ears!"[55]

19   But since the pleasure of taste makes many people prisoners of drink as much as of food, you must be careful not to become either a wine-bibber or a wine-fancier. Shun every intoxicating drink.[56] Drink moderately: satisfy your thirst, but don't let it cloud your mind.[57] Boys have a lot of juice: they are filled with milk and blood and rarely suffer thirst. Nothing is more shameful than a boy who craves wine. "The use of wine," as Valerius Maximus said, "was in former times unknown to Roman women."[58] What about boys? Shall we allow the minds of boys to become debauched, or shall we drown a growing intellect in unmixed wine? Although the Germanic custom makes it an act of impiety to mix water with wine, I shall never be persuaded that strong wine should be placed on boys' tables, unless weakened with water. I have been told that a certain Bohemian nobleman

used to accustom his children from infancy, even from the cradle itself, to large and frequent draughts of Malmsey or Rhenish wine exclusively. He would say: "Once they become men and start drinking in large quantities, no wine will be strong enough to knock them out." Perhaps Cyrus the Younger was reared this way: once, when urging the Spartans to form an alliance with him, he said that his heart was steadier than his brother's, for he himself drank more wine and held it better.[59] This is a foolish and vain precaution, always to be drunk so as never be drunk. Those who are nurtured this way, when they drink in quantity, do not lose consciousness, but the consciousness they have is that of a fool who is perpetually drunk. In this condition there is no memory, no liveliness of wit, no appetite for good literature, no zeal for glory or honor.

But lest we seem to be contending with beasts like these, whom   20
we consider it a crime to reckon amongst men, let us turn to Plato and hear that divine man's views about the drinking of wine. His wise belief was that wine should not be drunk indiscriminately, but that "by the proper and moderate relaxation of drinking the mind was refreshed and renewed for resuming the duties of sobriety." Not that the drinking of wine must be avoided entirely: no one can seem "truly continent or sufficiently faithful to temperance whose way of life is not tested amidst the perils of error and the allurements of pleasure. For when all the license and attractions of feasting are unknown and a man has had no experience of them, if perchance his will should bring him, accident lead him, or necessity compel him to experience pleasures of this kind," he will necessarily be "quickly captivated and bewitched by them, his mind and spirit unable to resist."[60] Therefore a boy must be fortified against the evil influence of wine, not by avoidance as the Egyptians do, nor by swilling as the Bohemians prefer, but by strength and continuous resolution of mind, so that through moderation he may become temperate and continent. We drink wine, not to

be mastered by it, but "to warm and refresh our minds, washing away any frigid severity or dull bashfulness."[61] This we will do when we take wine in moderate and tolerable quantities. Therefore let the banquets which take place in your presence be frugal with respect to food and drink, and constrained by special rules; and let them be sober and without luxury so as not to hinder the functions of either mind or body. Let there be no sadness or gloomy countenances there, but let laughter at times also be present. I do not praise Crassus who, Cicero writes, "smiled but once in his life,"[62] for in smiling the Savior exercised nothing but a human function. Let there be gravity in banqueting, but let it not exclude joyfulness. Let pleasures be present, but let them not lead to licentiousness.[63] Let there be musical entertainments, but let them not be accompanied by shamelessness.

21   But as we are still discussing the care of the body, that brief saying of Plato ought to be recalled: he would have the body be indulged only so far as was serviceable to philosophy. We think this a prudent dictum, providing we understand the care of the commonwealth to be included in the study of philosophy. For those who show the greatest solicitude for the body but overlook the soul, which ought to be served by the body, are no different from those who expend every effort to obtain the most perfect organs but neglect entirely the art [of organ-playing] for the sake of which such instruments are obtained. We must keep to the opposite course. We ought to chasten the body and hold in check its violent urges as if it were a savage beast, curbing with the rein of reason its reckless revolts against the soul. When Pythagoras learned that one of his friends was indulging in choice food in order to become fat, he said: "He is steadily constructing a more wretched prison for himself."[64] When Gnaeus Pompey, surnamed "the Great," was afflicted with ill health, his doctor ordered him to eat a thrush. His servants sought for one in vain, because they were not in season, and when one of his friends said that thrushes

could be found on the estate of Lucullus, who raised them year-round, Pompey, in spite of his sickness, replied: "Could Pompey not live, then, if Lucullus were not fond of his delicacies?"[65] and putting aside even modest preparation he took such food as was common and easily available.

The sole concern as regards food should be this: that the body should be supplied with the necessities that render it capable of enduring labor. Hence one must offer the belly sustenance, not pleasure. For those who are always worked up about dinners and cooks and who for the sake of a banquet scour every land and sea, are heavily burdened with miserable slavery and pay tribute to a most severe master. Their sufferings are not a whit less than the punishments of Hell: to cut up fire, to fetch water in a sieve, and strive to pour it into a perforated jar,[66] as Basil says.   22

You ask, perhaps, what I think of clothing and other bodily adornment. I shall say what I think should be done in a few words. To show more concern than necessary for one's hair or dress, as Diogenes says, is the mark of people who are either wretched or depraved. And so to be preoccupied with the adornment of the body is the mark of a trivial and entirely vain man, or of a man with designs on the chastity of virtuous wives and maidens. You must take care not to strive for superfluous effects, nor to allow more to the body than is healthy for the soul.[67] It would be shameful for a king to seem effeminate because of excessive attention to his body. But in all grooming of the body cleanliness must be maintained, not the kind that is annoying or foppish, but the kind that avoids rustic and barbarous negligence. It was a matter of reproach for Demosthenes and Hortensius that they were considered too neat, elegant, and fastidious in their dress and grooming habits. But in a boy or man of royal blood one must take account of dignity, so that in avoiding a reputation for ostentation he does not incur the infamous charge of avarice, than which nothing is more unattractive in a ruler.   23

24   Having finished this brief account of what we thought should be said on the care of the body, we now hasten on to the education of the mind. In this matter we would have you be persuaded that there is nothing men possess on earth more precious than intellect, and that the other goods of human life that we pursue with great effort are truly insignificant and unworthy. Nobility is beautiful but it is a good not one's own; riches are precious but they are the possession of fortune; glory is attractive but inconstant; beauty is becoming but fleeting and ephemeral; health is desirable but very much subject to change; strength is something one longs for but it becomes easily enfeebled in sickness or old age.

25   Nothing is more excellent than intellect and reason. These are things that no attack of fortune will take away, no slander will tear apart. And although all other goods are diminished by time, knowledge and reason increase with age. War carries away each possession and drives all before it; learning alone it is unable to snatch away. Once, after Demetrius had levelled conquered Megara to the ground, he asked the philosopher Stilpo, who was from Megara, whether he had lost anything that belonged to him. Stilpo replied, "Not at all: war takes no spoils from virtue." And when Gorgias inquired of Socrates whether he thought the king of the Persians was happy, Socrates replied: "I do not know how much virtue and knowledge he has," meaning that happiness endures because of the latter and not because of the goods of fortune.[68] Take this maxim and entrust it to your memory, King Ladislas, you who are destined to be extremely rich. Although great realms await you, you can still not be called happy unless you are endowed with virtue and your intellectual goods exceed the goods of fortune. For kingdoms and the wealth of the world are no more the property of their possessors than of anyone else, but, as in games of dice, they pass away and return now here, now there. The firm possession of virtue is alone unchangeable for the living and the dead, and Solon rightly said concerning riches,

"but we should not exchange riches for virtue."[69] Therefore, while riches pour down upon you, take care not to be wanting in virtue, for without the virtues no one deserves the name either of a king or of a man. As it is advantageous to lay up necessities for the winter during fine weather, so also good morals ought to be adopted in boyhood as the best provision for a virtuous old age.[70] Who knows the changeable fortunes of human life? Nothing is stable under the moon; now men are rich, now they are poor; now they rule, now they serve; now they rejoice in health, now they are sick. No one knows in the morning what the evening will bring.[71] No one has so many protecting deities that he may promise himself a morrow. For this reason Theseus, as Cicero says is related in Euripides, was accustomed to say,

> For remembering what I had heard from a learned man,
> I used to contemplate my future miseries,
> and was always planning either bitter death or the sad flight of
>   exile
> or some other grave evil,
> so that if any dread chance should bring calamity,
> no sudden care might torment me unprepared.[72]

But nothing offers a surer refuge against the attacks of a stepmotherly fortune than philosophy. Hence when the younger Dionysius, expelled from power and driven into exile, was asked what profit to him Plato and philosophy had been, he replied: "That I might bear with a tranquil and easy spirit just such a change of fortune."[73] Therefore whether circumstances are unpropitious or propitious to us, we ought to have recourse to philosophy, which is the study of virtue, and which kings especially should love.

A king, who (as Aristotle notes) is a kind of living law, has 26 many obligations.[74] The burden of government is great, for a king must strive not only to safeguard himself but also his people, to lead the multitude entrusted to him in accordance with justice into the way of security and peace. For it is written: "An unwise king scatters his people; a wise one enriches his cities."[75] Vegetius also says truly: "No one ought to have better or greater knowledge than a prince, whose prudence should profit all his subjects."[76] Thus when Solomon felt the burden of great responsibility on himself and had the chance to ask for whatever he wished from the Lord, he said: "Give Thy servant a docile heart that can judge Thy people and discern good and evil."[77] Moreover when Philip of Macedon was advising his son Alexander, he ordered him to heed Aristotle and devote himself to philosophy, adding, "Do not do many things of the sort I regret having done."[78]

27   You have already been persuaded, I think, that a boy destined to rule must study philosophy; but philosophy, the mother of all arts — which Plato thinks the gift of the gods, and Cicero their invention — cannot be readily comprehended without literary study. Philosophy will first educate you in divine worship, then in that human justice which is founded upon the association of the human race, then in modesty and greatness of soul; it will clear away the darkness from your soul as though from your eyes, so that you may see all that is above or below, the beginning, middle and end of everything.[79] Who therefore would be not be willing to toil over literature when such wonderful fruit is plucked from it? When it holds the knowledge of good and evil? When it tells our past, controls the present, and foretells the future? Every age without letters is dark, and an illiterate prince must depend on another's guidance. And since royal courts are filled with flatterers, who will speak the truth to the ruler? Is it not fitting that a king should have a liberal education, that he may garner truth for himself in the books of the philosophers? Indeed, Demetrius of Phalerum advised king Ptolemy to procure books dealing with kingdoms and empires and to read them thoroughly, for the things their friends do not dare advise them, kings will find written in books.[80]

Therefore the greatest attention and zeal must be devoted to   28
literature. But it has been asked at what age boys ought to begin
their studies. Hesiod thought not before the age of seven, since
that seemed the earliest age capable of instruction and labor;
Eratosthenes also held this view. But Aristophanes and Chrysippus, with whom Quintilian agrees, held that no time of life should
be free from study.[81] Training should begin in the very cradle; even
nurses should contribute their share to you. Chrysippus wanted
nurses to have sound judgment, if possible, so that no contagion
could be contracted from them, for bad habits stick to you more
tenaciously and good ones easily take a turn for the worse. The
words of a mother seasoned with patience and elegance have often
been profitable to sons; many have written of Cornelia, the mother
of the Gracchi, the fragrance of whose eloquence could be scented
in her sons.[82] It makes a great deal of difference whether mothers
or anyone else who raise boys are polished or coarse, prudent or
foolish. But you have now escaped from the yoke of your nurse; you
lost your mother, who was brilliant and unusually eloquent, before
you could know her. But let us put aside the past, more to be lamented than changed. Let us turn to your present time of life.

We trust that you were instructed as befits a Christian, that   29
you know the Lord's Prayer, the Ave Maria, the Gospel of John,
the Creed, also several collects, the names of the mortal sins, the
Gifts of the Holy Ghost, the Ten Commandments, the Works of
Mercy, and finally the way of saving the soul and leading it to
heaven. We do not doubt you are convinced that after this life
there is another which is joyful and sweet for the good, bitter and
full of trouble for the evil. Not only the Bible but also pagan literature shows this. Socrates, according to Cicero, argued that there
were two paths and two courses for souls departing from the body.
For those who had polluted themselves with human vices and
shameful deeds and surrendered themselves wholly to their lusts

or had committed outrageous crimes against the commonwealth, there was in the end a certain road cut off from the assembly of the gods. But for those who had kept themselves pure and chaste and imitated the life of the gods while in their human bodies, there lay open an easy return to those from whom they had departed.[83] What shall we say, we to whom the Gospels have been preached and who can seem to know, rather than merely believe, the incarnation of our Savior, confirmed by so many miracles? Indeed, if we are wise, we shall judge that this life of man is of no value at all, and we shall decide that nothing must be considered good which is not useful for the next life. And so in this life nothing can be called excellent: not rank, nor ancestry, nor strength of body, nor beauty, nor greatness, nor the honor of all mankind, nor even the empire itself. But our hopes must pass beyond these things; everything should be undertaken with a view to preparing for the next life. But to point out what this life is, or how it is lived, would be a greater task than we have undertaken for the present. Besides, to comprehend this matter requires an older scholar than you are. But let this one statement suffice: if someone imagines all the happiness since the creation of mankind and gathers it into one whole, he will in fact find that it equals only a small part of those [eternal] goods; that all human goods collected together are farther removed from the smallest good of that [eternal] life than shadows and dreams are from reality. The Holy Scriptures lead directly to this life, instructing us through hidden meanings. To this profound meaning you may not yet penetrate because of your age, yet it is not pointless for you to be trained in other books of learned men. For as Basil says: "We must apply ourselves to poets, orators, and other writers, and to all from whom we may derive profit in training the intellect."[84]

30   But since all literature repeatedly cries out that God must be worshipped beyond others, you must first of all give yourself and entrust yourself to Him; He is your Creator, your Father, and

your Lord; you owe everything to Him. And though all men ought to give thanks to God, *you* are obligated to be grateful in the highest degree and to serve Him through whose bounty you have been born a king. You could have been born a commoner or a peasant, but the inscrutable judgment of God has placed you upon a lofty throne. You should not be elated, nor swollen with pride, nor arrogant, because what has been given to you might have been given to another. The nobler your birth, the more humbly you ought to conduct yourself, bowing before religion, and assisting at divine offices. All else easily waits upon him to whom divine worship is dear. "Seek ye first the kingdom of God," says Holy Scripture, "and after this all things shall be added unto you."[85] Although the Romans were pagans, they held that all things must be placed second to religion; even in those rites wherein they wanted the honor due highest majesty to be conspicuous, the imperial powers did not hesitate to subject themselves to religious rites, believing that in this way they would rule over human affairs, if they had well and faithfully served the divine power.[86] What must *we* do, who know the true God?

Do not think that religion is subject to you, even though you enjoy the name of a great prince. Not the lord, but the son of the Church, it is you who are subject to the authority of the priesthood in the things that belong to God. Although the emperor Theodosius was very powerful and governed the Roman empire, he still bowed his head before Ambrose, bishop of the Church of Milan, and humbly performed the penance imposed upon him. Constantine always displayed the greatest reverence for the priesthood; he did not wish to give judgment over the bishops at the Council of Nicaea, saying that gods should not be judged by men.[87] And no wonder, for Clement, who succeeded Saint Peter in the apostolic office, says in a letter of his that all the rulers of the earth and all men ought to be obedient or bow their heads before priests, but that the latter should be judged by the Lord alone,

31

for they are His and not another's. And who is it who should judge the servant of another? If men do not permit this, neither shall the God of gods and the Lord of lords in any wise permit it. Thus preached St. Peter, the keeper of the keys of eternal life, according to that holy bishop.[88] You therefore shall honor priests, God's servants, and shall not allow them to be oppressed, burdened, or afflicted with injustice of any kind. You shall not say that a priest is foolish, unworthy, or impure. This is not your business; he has his judge; whatever crime he commits will not go unpunished. You will respect their dignity and their sacrament, and you will not listen to peevish and wicked youths who try to persuade you otherwise with flattery.

32   At this point we must make clear what sort of youths we would have associate with you, and what sort of boys it is just and sensible to have in your service; for from them both harm and benefit can accrue. For this reason let those who assist you be instructed in good morals; let there be no vice in them; let them employ no foul language, for we are all prone to imitate shameful and corrupt ways; as an old proverb has it, if you live near a lame person, you will sometimes limp yourself, too.[89]

Habit is strong in tender years,

as Vergil says.[90] But let your tutors take care that no youth who is a flatterer associate with you.[91] For they are a pernicious race of men who praise whatever they hear praised, then curse with whoever curses. If somebody denies, they deny; and whenever they hear someone affirming, they affirm; and as the octopus changes its color according to the appearance of the soil beneath it, so they vary their views in accordance with the pleasure of their audience, prepared to bear witness against justice and against God, if they think it will please their listener.[92] Let this plague be driven from your dwelling! But let truthful boys be in your company, upright,

chaste, and votaries of modesty and holiness; neither false, nor de-
ceivers, nor obstinate, neither drunkards nor sots, nor unjust.

Let some of them know Hungarian, some Bohemian, some   33
your native tongue, but all should know the Latin language, and
let them speak in turn. Thus you will learn all these individual
languages without labor as if in play, and you will be able to address your subjects directly. Nothing wins the favor of a people towards their prince more than graceful speech. The ruler who does
not understand his people when they are complaining or request-
ing something is in a sense unworthy of his kingdom. The knowledge of many languages was as advantageous to your maternal
grandfather, a well-loved king, as the lack of such knowledge
was harmful to your father. Who does not commend Mithridates,
the king of Pontus, who spoke without an interpreter with the
twenty-two nations over whom he ruled?[93] And I would not have
you more dear to the Austrian people than to the Bohemian and
Hungarian; all your peoples must be governed with equal zeal. As
Plato says, he does an unjust act who cares for one part of the
commonwealth to such an extent that he neglects the other.[94] This
has very frequently been the cause of great disasters for princes.
And this is the most important reason why the most noble province of Italy withdrew from the empire; for the Teutonic kings,
content with their native land alone and attached too much to
their firesides, neglected the government of Italy. Love safeguards
kingdoms no less than the sword, but it is impossible to love the
man who does not love. The commerce of language is the intermediary of love. Therefore while your age permits, you must strive to
be able to listen your subjects on your own, to understand them,
and to speak with them. Frequently matters arise which your subjects may wish to refer to you alone and which they would not entrust to an interpreter. A prince, moreover, who always speaks
through another deserves the name of ruled more than that of

ruler. Silence, as Homer says, brings honor to a woman, but it does not to a man.[95]

34   Now since speech comes from practice, we think that something must be said about the manner in which the faculty of speech should be formed in a boy, so that when he has arrived at man's estate he can not only speak, but speak elegantly and wisely, an accomplishment no one thinks a king should neglect. Those who excel others in the art of speaking procure the greatest praise for themselves. And this was the one art that gave Ulysses, though unwarlike, mastery over the combative Ajax. For after Achilles was slain, it was not the strong arm but the flowery tongue that carried off his weapons. Therefore the criticism is quite wrong that some make of Cicero's famous saying, "let arms yield to the toga, let laurels yield to the tongue,"[96] for as he also says: "Since men differ from beasts in that they can speak, what praise, then, is worthy of the man who excels other men in the very skill by which men excel beasts?"[97] But although we approve the speech of an educated tongue more than the habits of a silent prince, still we do not advise a boy to speak without forethought, for what is said or done inconsiderately or rashly cannot be lovely. Unpremeditated speeches of men (to say nothing of boys) are full of shallowness and carelessness, while thoughtful preparation prevents digression. But why speak of boys when the renowned orators, Pericles and Demosthenes, very often refused to address the people because they said that they were unprepared? Indeed, if anyone allows boys to speak *ex tempore*, he lays the foundations of extreme garrulity. I would not have too much freedom of speech be extended to you as a boy; a seasonable silence is the mark of great wisdom, and not infrequently there are more people who regret having given an outstanding speech than there are those who regret having kept silence. What is kept in silence is easily brought forth; but there is no way to recall what has once been uttered.[98] For as Horace says: "A word, once let out, flies beyond recall."[99]

What therefore shall we say when there is so much that is   35
advantageous both in silence and in speech? We would have you
hold to a middle course:[100] be neither always silent nor always
speaking. We do not demand a Pythagorean silence of five years'
duration, nor the loquacity of Thersites.[101] The ancients used to
say that the tongue ought not to be free and wandering, but
moved and, as it were, governed by chains linked to the depths of
one's heart and spirit.[102] For it is reasonable to conclude that the
speech of facile, shallow, vain, and importunate speakers is born in
the mouth and not in the spirit. On the contrary, Homer said that
Ulysses uttered words endowed with shrewd eloquence, not from
his mouth but from his breast. To be sure the rampart of the teeth
was set to check the heedlessness of words, that rashness in speaking might be restrained not only by the guardianship of the heart,
but also hedged about by sentinels, as it were, placed in the
mouth.[103] But be careful that that saying of Epicharmus is not
thrown up against you: "a man who could not be silent, though he
could not speak;"[104] nor that of Sallust: "a voluble person rather
than an eloquent one."[105] It is necessary that the powers of speech
take root, and then, when the moment demands it, freedom to
speak may be granted. Too much silence takes away the faculty of
speaking. For just as those who have been confined in chains for a
long time are unable to walk after being freed because they have
become used to their chains, so those who have restrained their
speech too long are struck dumb if ever they should have to speak
unexpectedly.[106]

But something should be said about what is appropriate for a   36
boy, so that you may form your powers of speech correctly. In the
first place your voice must be formed; let it not break with feminine shrillness, nor tremble like an old man's, nor bellow too much
like a cow. Let the words be pronounced and let each letter be
enunciated with its proper sound; don't let the final syllables be
cut off; don't let the voice be heard in the throat[107] and let your

tongue be ready, your face relaxed, and your speech expressive. Your teachers will offer you certain words and verses of studied difficulty, consisting of many syllables coming together in a very harsh way, all jammed together and clashing, so that you may reel them off, pronouncing them as swiftly as possible.[108] Even Demosthenes, since he was slow of tongue, used to place pebbles in his mouth and recite his speeches alone; then, after taking them out, he would speak in the senate with great fluency and polish.[109]

37   Once you have received instruction in these rules, you will strive to overcome your contemporaries in beauty and gravity of speech. May you strive to emerge the victor both in this and in every praiseworthy endeavor! Defeat will pain you, victory will give you joy. For although ambition is itself a vice, it frequently has been the cause of virtue.[110] And the boy cannot be too much commended whom praise arouses, who weeps when conquered, whom glory delights.[111]

38   Let there be no baseness in any speech of yours, since, as Democritus says, speech is the shadow of an action,[112] and as the Apostle says, "evil conversations corrupt good morals"[113] — a saying, Jerome notes, which is taken from Menander.[114] And since merry speeches generally contain some hidden evil, as poisons are drunk mixed with honey, during every evil speech one should imitate Ulysses, who placed wax in his ears so as not to hear the Sirens' songs.[115] Let there be ease in conversation, pleasantness in hailing those we meet, and kindness in answering, for a heavy manner in conversation draws upon oneself merited dislike. Let pertinacity be absent from your disputes; let prudence conquer and reason hold sway. It is an attractive trait not only to win, but also to know how to lose. We should accept the view of Euripides, who affirms that in a dispute between two men, when one becomes enraged, far wiser is the one who curbs his tongue.[116] Let your words contain no injustice, no falsehoods, for lying is a slavish vice which all mortals ought to hunt down with hatred.[117] The

greater the rank of the man who lies, the more detestable his wickedness. For Juvenal says that

> every vice has a more egregious criminality about it
> the greater the reputation of the man who sins.[118]

Moreover, let your speech not be too humble nor servile, nor yet proud nor arrogant. Haughty speech is uncivil, plain speech fails to inspire. Just as the body should not only have soundness but even a fine carriage, so too it is fitting that speech be not only not weak but even vigorous.[119] These are greater matters than you can comprehend, but they will be clear to you in time. And grammar will direct this material of speech which nature supplies, dialectic will sharpen it, rhetoric will embellish it, and philosophy will season and perfect it. Something will be said of these arts in the proper place.

But since the ability to speak—to name words and thoughts simultaneously—cannot exist without the help of memory, there is need for a boy to exercise his memory. A good memory is a sign of intelligence in children, and such a memory has threefold virtues: it perceives effortlessly, it retains faithfully, and it imitates with ease.[120] Something must be committed to memory daily, whether verses or important maxims from illustrious authors.[121] For memory is called the storeroom of knowledge and learning, and in the fables it is called the mother of the Muses because it begets and nourishes. You should strengthen it in two respects whether you possess a naturally good memory or a bad one. For you should either reinforce your abundance or supply your defects, obeying the verses of Hesiod, who spoke as follows:

> If you strive to add small things to tiny ones
> and do that frequently, a huge pile is accumulated.[122]

But because grammar is known to be the gateway of every discipline and holds more within than it displays outwardly, and can

39

40

seem hopelessly difficult unless it it is learned in boyhood and youth, we wish to advise you briefly not to despise this art as unworthy of the lofty heights of royalty. There is nothing harmful in grammar except what is superfluous. We know that the greatest men were devoted students of it. Marcus Tullius Cicero, the orator, consul and preserver of his country, showed this in the letters written to his son. Julius Caesar, the great general, was so devoted to this art that he wrote a faultless book *On Analogy*.[123] Also Octavian Augustus showed how skilled he was in grammar in letters written to that same Caesar, since, as Quintilian testifies, he prefers the more correct form *calidum* to *caldum*, not because the latter is not Latin but because it is disagreeable.[124] So do not be ashamed to learn what the greatest princes in the world strove with great zeal to obtain. We have said above that learning is necessary for kings, but if you have little faith in me, let the royal prophet advise you: "And now, kings, understand," he enjoins, "receive instruction, you that judge the earth."[125] But how can you learn and receive instruction unless you receive the beginning and foundation of all learning, which is grammar? So far, you have devoted effort to this art and you have listened willingly to the advice of your teacher. Nevertheless, you have not as yet become a finished grammarian, for you still are in the process of learning. Hence we have decided to write something about grammar for you, not because we ourselves wish to teach you grammar, but that we may point out briefly the fountains from whose draughts true grammarians are made, and to which, we hope, your teachers may lead you, the more so as we believe this to be highly beneficial to you.

41   *Grammatica*, as Quintilian says, means "literature" when translated into Latin, and has three parts: the science of correct speech, the explanation of the poets and other authors, and composition.[126] Let us touch somewhat on all of these areas; that will be useful for you to hear and not unpleasant for us to discuss. The

first part is the science of correct speech. By speaking correctly, we understand here that speech which is pronounced in words duly joined and connected, although it might in other respects be harmful, impudent, or less than just. If, therefore, we wish to speak grammatically and correctly, we must learn the use of words, of which some are native to us, some foreign; some simple, some compound; some proper, some metaphorical; some in common use, some coinages.[127] The whole power of correct speaking turns on these distinctions, on the apt choice and arrangement of words.

All words are called "native" which were invented by the Italic 42 peoples, such as *amor*, *lectio*, and *scriptio*. "Foreign" words are those received from all neighboring nations, such as *raeda* from the Gauls, *gurdi* (i.e., persons commonly believed to be stupid) from the Spaniards and *marchio* from the Germans; but an infinite number come from the Greeks, from whom Roman speech is so largely derived. And indeed in Greek words the Latin declension must be used so far as decorum permits, so that we say *Plato* and *Palaemo*, not *Platon* and *Palaemon*, because the Latin nominative does not usually end in *-on*.[128] Yet it is not absurd that the Greek declension is also sometimes found, especially in poetry, as in Vergil:

Only let *Palaemon* who is even now coming hear this[129]
. . . . .
and the same *Alcimedon* gave two goblets to us
. . . . .
he placed *Orphea* in their midst[130]

and

I love *Phyllida* beyond others[131]

and

they would pour libations of wine in the midst of the *aulai* [hall].[132]

93

The ancients did not permit Greek masculine nouns to end in -as in the nominative, and therefore in many writers we find *Aenea, Pelia, Euthia*, and *Hermagora*.[133] But now it would be a mistake if you don't say *Peleas, Aeneas, Eutheias*, and *Hermagoras*, as the Greek declension has now entered Latin usage.

43   "Simple" words are *amo, lego, probus, territus*, and words like them. "Compound" words are *adamo, perlego, improbus*, and *perterritus*. Sometimes compounds are formed from two words, as *perterritus* from *per* and *territus*, sometimes from three, as *imperterritus* from *in, per*, and *territus*; similarly, *compositus* and *incompositus*. Cicero thinks that *capresis* is also formed from three words, that is, *cape, si*, and *vis*; and there are those who interpret the *lupercalia* as *ludere per caprum*. And words are joined either from two complete Latin words, as *superfui* and *subterfui*, although it might be asked whether they are compounded from complete words; or from complete and corrupt, as *malivolus*; or from corrupt and complete, as *noctivagus*; or from two corrupt words, as *pedissequus*; or from a native word and a foreign word, as *biclinium*; or the opposite, as *antiato*; or from two foreign words, as *epiraedia* and *antichristus*. For *epi* is a Greek preposition, *raeda* a "Gallic chariot," yet neither Greek nor Gaul would say *epiraedium*. The Romans made their word from both foreign words.

44   Those words are called "proper" which preserve their original meaning,[134] as *flumen* (that which is always flowing with a supply of water) and *torrens* (that which is swollen in time of flood and fails in drought). And there is need of no small diligence in knowing and placing these words correctly, so that we say *aedem* for the temple of God, *aedes* for the home of a great man, and not the opposite; or so that we employ *labor* for *dolor* or *dolor* for *labor*.

45   Words are said to be "transferred" [or metaphorical] which have one meaning by nature, another derived from their context, as *gemma* signifies by its nature a precious stone, but, transferred from one context to another, it can signify a droplet which a

pruned vine will often extrude, or a budding sprout in the early spring. A word is transferred from its original context into another where it either loses its proper meaning or its "transferred" meaning seems better than its proper one. Either necessity or utility compels us to transfer words. Necessity [compels us] in the case of the word *gemma* of which we have already spoken, for the farmer did not have any other name by which to call the budding branch or the drop of liquid extruding from the vinestem. It is because of necessity also that we call a man *durus* and *asper*, because we have no proper word to designate these dispositions. Utility may be subdivided into two, for we use metaphorical senses as either more meaningful or more elegant than the proper senses. It is more meaningful when we say that a man is "incensed with anger," "inflamed with passion," or "has slipped into error;"[135] it would have been proper but less rich in meaning to say "an angry man," "a passionate man," or "an erring man." As a rule, many metaphorical terms are introduced for the sake of elegance, such as "the light of speech," "distinction of descent," "the storms of the assembly," and "the thunder of eloquence."[136] While a moderate and seasonable use of metaphorical terms adorns one's speech, frequent and excessive use of them renders it obscure and tedious; and extended use of metaphor leads to allegory and enigmas.[137] No small degree of judgment is needed to recognize what counts as an over-extended or inelegant metaphor. To me that seemed a good and pleasant metaphor when St. Augustine in his sermon on the Holy Innocents said: "Who with justice are called the flowers of the martyrs, whom the frost of persecution caused to waste away like the first bursting buds of the Church after they had sprung forth in the midst of the cold of infidelity."[138] Cicero thought that to speak of the state as being "castrated by the death of Africanus"[139] was inept. What if he had heard the man who said that a parrot "coins" words because it tries to imitate our voices?

46   Words are "common" which are worn down through general use, and these we can more safely employ. As Cicero says, words that were harsh at first become softened by use, and in his day the word "urbane"[*urbanus*] was no longer a daring expression, nor was the word "piratical" [*piratica*] in Quintilian's lifetime;[140] today these are trite. Who amongst the ancients would have said *scandalum* or *gehenna*? But the Gospel text has handed these words down to us. Hence that saying of Horace is confirmed:

> Many words will be reborn which have now fallen into disuse,
> and many will perish which are now in good form
> if usage shall wish it so — usage, which with opinion is the law
>   and norm of speaking.[141]

47   "Coined" words are those which someone newly invents for himself, as in Horace, *inimicat urbes*,[142] "he enemies cities" i.e., "he makes cities enemies." Again, he seems to coin a word in another place: "He retarded [*tardo*] the speedy wings of fate,"[143] i.e., "delayed." Servius says that once upon a time it was customary for priests to be emasculated with certain herbs so that they could no longer have intercourse.[144] This word *emasculare* was formed from *ex* and *masculo*. But not everyone may form new words. As Horace remarks:

> It has been and always will be allowable
> to produce a word marked with the stamp of the present day;
> as the forests with their leaves are changed in the declining
>   year
> and the first leaves fall, so the archaic usage of words perishes
> and other words are duly born afresh, flourish and become
>   vigorous.[145]

But this prerogative should belong to those who have made a great name for themselves as speakers and writers, such as Terence, who first said *obsequium* [devoted service], and Messala, who invented the word *reatus* [defendant], and Augustus, who first thought up *munerarius* [a giver of public shows].[146] Those who are of mediocre ability should not invent words but should use those that others have invented. There should be no honor or praise in the use of any word, whether new or old, native or foreign, proper or metaphorical, unless those words are well adapted to their objects. And when there is a choice of two expressions, it is preferable to use the one which is more euphonious and more easily understood; for example, you should say *beatitudo* rather than *beatitas*.[147]

Now that we have learned about the nature of words, we need to master diminutives, inflections, and derivations. You should not be surprised that *scabellum* [little stool] comes from *scamnus* [stool], *villa* [a country residence] from *vinum* [wine], *pusillus* [tiny] from *parvus* [small], *bipennis* [a double-edged ax] comes from *pinna* [feather]; that from the nominative *bos* [cow] comes [the accusative] *bovem*, and that from *lavando* [washing] come *lotum* and *illotum* [washed and unwashed]. Words vary greatly in their cases, tenses, numbers, and moods, and these variations have been passed down by our grammarians in great detail. A preposition when joined to a verb sometimes changes the vowel, as *cadit: excidit, caedit: excidit, calcat: exculcat* bear witness.[148] There have been people who believed that the word *pepigi* comes from *paciscor* [I agree to], but this is entirely untrue, for *paciscor* forms its preterite tense, *pactus sum*, from itself, and not *pepigi*. The latter, Quintilian affirms, comes from *pago* [to agree to something].[149] For *pagunt* is found in the Twelve Tables and *cadunt* is similar to it; but the latter comes from *cado*, and so therefore also *pagunt* from *pago*. *Cado* has the preterite *cecidi*; *pago* has *pepigi*.[150] We must add gender to this: you should not call feminine nouns masculine nor common nouns neuter. Next — and more important — you should learn about the agreement of verbs and nouns. One must know

48

97

how to place pronouns and participles suitably, and adverbs, prepositions, and interjections should not be neglected. Finally, one must take the utmost pains that no verbal utterance is disgraced by the presence of barbarisms or solecisms.

49   Barbarism in fact flows from multiple sources: from race, as when African, Spanish or German words not in Latin usage are mixed with Latin speech; from nature, for when you talk in an insolent, menacing or cruel way you appear to be speaking like a barbarian; and from interchange of words, as when you subtract, add or vary syllables or letters, or change their order, for example when Tinga Placentinus said *precula* for *pergula* and was stigmatized by Hortensius for committing a double barbarism. Yet among the writers of verse barbarisms often deserve pardon or even praise,[151] as in Vergil:

> *nec spes libertatis erat, nec cura peculi.*[152]

Here he uses *peculi* for *peculii*, and in another place,

> *cingite fronte coma et pocula porgite dextris,*[153]

he has *porgite* for *porrigite*. And Juvenal, adding a syllable, speaks thus of Nero:

> *qualis tunc epulas ipsum gluttisse putemus*
> *induperatorem,*[154]

because the meter did not allow the word *imperatorem*. There are certain words which, when expressed separately, are mistakes, but are unobjectionable if joined to other words: *dua, tre,* and *pondo* smack of barbarism, but *duapondo* and *trepondo* are correct, says Quintilian. It is a barbarism to pronounce as short a syllable that is long, or to lengthen a short syllable. This privilege is sometimes extended to poets,[155] as in

> *Italiam fato profugus Laviniaque venit,*[156]

where Vergil makes the first syllable long, although it is universally short.

We also commit the fault of solecism in many ways, as when 50 the proper gender of something is not given, for example when you say *hunc arborem, arbor* being feminine. Yet we can say *corticem amaram* or *amarum*, since Vergil is an authority for both. It is a solecism if a verb, participle, or preposition is not assigned its proper case. If, when calling a single person to you, you say *venite* [come ye]; or if, when dismissing several, you say *abi* [leave thou]; or if you answer someone asking *quem video* [whom do I see?] by *ego*,[157] you will be guilty of solecism. If you say that you possess a *magnum peculiolum* [a large little property] or a *grandem equulum* [a large little horse], your diction is improper, but you are not committing a solecism.[158] *An* and *aut* are both conjunctions; yet if you ask *hic aut ille fuerit* [Is this or that person here?], you fall into error.[159] No less will you err if instead of *ne feceris*, you say *non feceris*, for although *ne* and *non* are both adverbs, one is the adverb of negation, the other of prohibition.[160] Still, in the Bible one finds *non furtum feceris* [161] [do not steal], where theft is being prohibited, but there also, as in the poets, many things are said with greater freedom than precision. There are some words used only in the singular, some only in the plural, while some are declined in a few cases only. Changes of case can involve solecism, for one cannot say either *nex mihi instat* [death threatens me] or *mortes imminent* [deaths threaten], although this latter may sometimes be permitted if reference is being made to several persons.[162] For one person can die only one death. Nor should we say *paterno mani sacra facio* [I perform sacrifices for the paternal spirit], but *paternis manibus*.[163] Yet some expressions have the appearance of solecism which are nevertheless not erroneous, as *tragedia Thyestes, ludi Floria,* and *Megalensia stemmata*; these are attested more frequently among the poets to be sure, but are also permitted to orators. There are also feminine names used by males, such as Sulla, Catilina, Jugurtha, Messala,

Galla, Dolabella, and Agrippa, and neuter names used by women,[164] such as Glycerium, Dorcium, Philorcium, and Eustochium; these are not mistakes.

51   If anyone wishes to avoid faults in all these instances, it will be necessary for him to know the four principles which grammatical speech recognizes: reason [or logic], antiquity, authority, and custom. Let us begin with reason.

52   Reason as understood by grammarians springs from analogy and etymology.[165] And yet in these sciences reason is less important than example, because both are subject to custom. People who obstinately adhere to etymologies and analogies more than to custom are therefore foolish: for example, people who would say *audaciter* rather than *audacter*, *conire* rather than *coire*, and *frugalis* rather than *frugi*, even though all the orators follow the latter usages.

53   Analogy translated from Greek into Latin is called "proportion," and can be called an argument from similarity. Its power comes from comparing something doubtful with something similar to it about which there is no doubt, so that we may prove the uncertain by the certain. For example, when it is asked whether *funis* is masculine or feminine, the word may be compared to *panis*. If there is doubt whether we should say *hac domu* or *hac domo*, *anus* and *manus* provide analogies. If you want to know whether *ferveo*, *ferves* makes *fervere* with a short or long syllable, there will be words analogous to them like *prandeo*, *spondeo*, and *pendeo* which form *prandere*, *spondere*, and *pendere*, keeping the middle syllable long. But one can be deceived a great deal when using analogies. In Lucilius one finds

> *fervit aqua et fervet: fervit nunc, fervet ad annum*
> Water boils and will boil: now it boils, it will boil for a year,

as if [the word were conjugated] *fervo*, *fervis*, *fervit*.[166] Vergil also had the middle syllable short in

fervere litora late
the seacoasts boil far and wide.[167]

We usually say *in domo fuimus* [we were at home], not *in domu*.
Lupus and *lepus* are no less analogous than *panis* and *funis*, yet *lepus*
is of common gender, while *lupus* is masculine, although Varro
says that *lupus* is feminine, following Ennius and Fabius Pictor.[168]

Etymology, which seeks the origin of words, requires much   54
learning. Some have called it *notatio*, others *veriloquium*, but those
who have examined the force of the word more closely say
originatio. Marcus Caelius gives an example of it in his own person:
he wanted to prove that he was "frugal" *[homo frugi]*, not on the
grounds that he was temperate (for he could not dissemble on *that*
point), but because he was useful to many, that is, *fructuosus* [fruit-
ful],[169] the source of the word *frugalitas*. Some who are overly devoted to etymology strive to bring back to their proper senses
words that have been altered somewhat in various and manifold
ways, having had their letters or syllables shortened or lengthened,
added to or subtracted from or exchanged. So much is this the
case that weak intellects sometimes fall into the most shameful ab-
surdities, like those who think that man is called *homo* because he
was born on the ground *[humus]*, as though the first mortals would
have given a name to the land before they gave one to themselves.[170] For although, as Genesis says, God gave a name to the
dry land, He did not call it *humus*, but *terra*;[171] the word *humus*
arose later. Some foolishly consider that *verba* [words] is derived
from *aere verberato* [beaten air], and that *stella* [star] is from *luminis
stilla* [drop of light], and that *caelibes* [bachelors] are like *caelites* [in-
habitants of heaven], because they are free from a heavy burden,[172]
and that *Vienna* was so called from *bienna* [two years], because for
two years it withstood a siege by Julius Caesar; yet in Caesar's lifetime it had not yet been founded, and at first it was not called *Vienna*, but *Flaviana [castra]*. But who shall not be excused when, as

Quintilian attests, even great Varro was mistaken? For he thinks that "field" *[agrum]* was so called because "something is driven in it" *[aliquid agatur]*, and that "jackdaws" *[graculi]* were so named because they fly "in a flock" *[gregatim]*. But Quintilian declares that the former comes from the Greek and the latter are named from their cries. And there are many people who believe that the *merula* [blackbird] is so called because it "flies unmixed" *[mera volans]*.[173] But no etymologies are to be accepted unless they have been approved by famous orators or parade an obvious derivation, as *consul* from *consulendo* [consulting] or *iudicando* [judging], for the ancients called judging "consulting" *[consulere]*. Hence the expression, "he pleads that you consult the good of" *[rogat ut boni consulas]*, i.e., that you be satisfied with something.[174] Do not miss the point that etymology, as was said above, is subordinate to custom; hence we say *triquetra Sicilia*, not *triquadra*, and *meridies*, not *medidies*.[175]

55   A certain majesty imparts a kind of religious attractiveness to old words. Words recovered from antiquity not only have great champions, but they also confer a rather delightful gravity upon one's speech. Since they are unfamiliar and also have the authority of antiquity, they give birth to a charm similar to novelty. But care must be taken to use them neither too often nor too obviously — because nothing is more detestable than affectation — nor to go hunting for them in times far distant and forgotten.[176] We ought to remember Favorinus the philosopher, who, as is recorded in Aulus Gellius's *Attic Nights*, addressed a young man very fond of words who in his ordinary daily speech used to produce many expressions that were too unfamiliar and archaic, saying: "Curius, Fabricius, and Coruncanius, men of olden days, and the Horatian triplets, who were of a still greater antiquity, talked clearly and intelligibly with their companions, nor do we find that they used any foreign expressions of the Aurunci or the Sicani, who are said to have first inhabited Italy; they spoke the language of their day. But

you would speak now as though addressing Evander's mother; you would use a diction that has been obsolete these many years because you want no one to know or understand what you are saying. Why not accomplish your purpose more fully, you silly fellow, and say nothing at all? But you say that antiquity is pleasing to you, because it is honorable, good, sober, and chaste. Live by all means according to the customs of the past, but speak in the language of the present, and always remember and take to heart what Caesar, a man of great talent and wisdom, wrote in the first book of his treatise *On Analogy*: 'Avoid as you would a rocky promontory a strange and unfamiliar word.'"[177] Let moderation therefore be employed, lest words recovered from antiquity be too frequent, too obscure, or entirely obsolete. For who would now say *nox* for *nocte*, or *im* for *eum*? But the Twelve Tables have this, for it was thus written there: *si nox furtum factum fuerit; si im occiderit jure caesus esto.*[178]

Authority [for Latin usage] is usually based on the orators or 56
the historians, and equally on the poets when their metrical form does not require one thing rather than another. For example: *Immo de stirpe decisum,* and *aëriae quo congessere palumbes,* and *silice in nuda.*[179] From these passages we learn that *stirps* is of the masculine, *palumbes* and *silex* of the feminine gender, since metrical necessity did not require any change of gender. But the judgement of the greatest men in the field of eloquence often takes the place of logic; the error of those following great leaders is, as it were, an honest one;[180] but we must be careful not to imitate authors that are too ancient or too obscure. Indeed, although it might seem that those who use words handed down in the very best authors are above reproach, it is still of capital importance to notice not only what they said but also how persuasive they proved to be. Since clarity is the highest power of speech, surely speech that requires an interpreter is very much flawed.[181] Who would now say

noctu concubia and *hac noctu filo pendebit Etruria tota*,[182] although Ennius is the author of both utterances? Who would say *lurcina-bundum* as Cato did, or *gladiola* with Messala?

57   There remains custom, then, the most certain teacher of the art of speaking, before which reason, antiquity, and all authority give way. We must employ speech like money, using the common currency. It would be utterly ridiculous to prefer the language men used to speak to the language they speak now.[183] Logic once demanded that we say *invidere te* just as we say *videre te* — indeed, Accius actually said this in his *Melanippus: quisnam florem liberum invidit meum?*[184] All the same, Cicero says this is prohibited by custom.[185] *Iduare*, from which the Ides are said to come, the ancient Etruscans said was the same as *dividere* [divide], whence comes *vidus* [widow], as if it were really *idua*, i.e., "divided"[186] or separated from her husband. Today no one would say *iduare*, although custom has left us *Idus* and *viduas*. Nor would anyone dare write *diequinte* or *diequinti* joined together as adverbs, although endorsed by the authority of Pomponius' verse, from the Atellan farce entitled *Mevia*:

> *Dies hic tertius, cum nihil egi: diequarte moriar fame.*
> For three days now I've done no work; on the fourth day I'll
>   die of hunger.

It is the same story with *die pristini*:[187] on the authority of some ancient writers who were not without learning, this expression is attested as signifying *die pristino*, i.e., "the previous day," or *pridie* as is now said,[188] custom approving the latter more than the former.

58   But here, too, good judgment is necessary so as not to slip into vulgar usage. In the first place we must determine what it is that we are calling "custom." For if what the greater number do is to be called custom, that will yield a dangerous principle, as Quintilian says, not only for one's diction but, more importantly, for one's life. For where would so much goodness come from that the many

should approve of what is right? Wisdom is found not in the many but in the few, and eloquence belongs not to a people but to a handful of men. Vast is the number of men who fuss over the length and cut of their hair, who carouse at the baths,[189] who are devoted to dining out, who are slaves to pleasure and unlawful gain; those who abstain from these things are few. Heaven forbid that we should imitate the former; let us flee such men. And how many there are who pervert the Latin language! For *amare* [to love] and *insequi Veneris cupiditate feminas* [to pursue women with venereal desire], the people of this land say *hovizare*; "expenses arising from a journey," they call *ceralia*; when they want to indicate that someone will come, they do not say *veniet* but *erit cito venire*. Well then, shall we follow men like these because they are in the majority and take our linguistic customs and usage from the multitude? Send this error on its way! That must not be accepted as a norm of language which has become implanted erroneously in however great a number: correct usage comes from good behavior, not from vice. Therefore just as in life correct usage must appeal to and imitate the consensus of good men, so also in speech correct usage must appeal to and imitate the agreement of the learned.[190]

We have not belabored but have rather indicated somewhat   59
briefly and summarily for your benefit the springs of the first part of grammar. From these your teachers can and should have you drink, explaining to you the books of Priscian and others who have spoken with exactness of judgement and expression. Meanwhile, I shall bring before us the second part of grammar and consider what it is.

The disciplines are interconnected, and a person cannot master   60
one unless he seeks light from another. Indeed, no one possesses the art of correct speaking who has not looked at the poets and read the historians and orators. Where else may one learn whatever there is of logic, antiquity, authority and custom in the art of grammar? For this reason, the second portion of grammar re-

quires not only that the aforementioned authors be read and understood, but that all classes of articulate and reputable writers should be considered, not only for the sake of their learning but also for their vocabulary, which frequently borrows its force from authoritative writers.[191] Therefore it is advantageous and necessary that your teachers display no little industry in collecting, considering, and explaining them to you.

61   The ancients laid it down that one's readings should commence with Homer and Vergil, even though more mature judgment is needed to comprehend their virtues. But there is plenty of time to acquire that; these authors will be read more than once. In the meantime, the child's mind will be exalted by the sublimity of heroic verse, and he will be inspired by great affairs and endowed with the noblest sentiments,[192] as Augustine, too, notes approvingly in the first book of his *City of God*.[193] I do not see how you can learn Greek, since no teacher of this subject is at hand. But I *will* say that you should acquire this language, if the opportunity presents itself. A knowledge of Greek—which not a few of the greatest Western emperors possessed—would be of no small help in ruling the kingdom of Hungary, which has many Greeks dwelling nearby, and would shed much light on Latin diction. For with me the authority of great Cato, who even as an old man devoted himself to Greek letters, prevails over that of Gaius Marius, who thought it disgraceful to learn a language whose teachers were slaves.[194] We have the will to learn Greek, but lack the resources, so let us speak about Latin literature. Latin literature we possess in sufficient abundance so that with its help we can acquire a very rich and elegant Latin diction.

62   Soon, however, the throng of those who wish to seem, rather than be[195] theologians will revile me because I am about to speak of the poets and urge the reading of them. "Why do you bring poets to us from Italy," they will say, "and why do you hasten to corrupt the holy morals of Germany with the effeminate licentious-

ness of the poets? Was not Marcus Nobilior branded as shameful by your Romans for bringing the poet Ennius into Aetolia when he was consul?[196] Did not your Cicero, whom you follow, whom you admire, say in his *Tusculan Disputations* that the poets were rightly banished by Plato from his imaginary state, since he required the best morals and the best condition for his republic?[197] What about Boethius? Did he not call the Muses of the poets "prostitute actresses?"[198] What about St. Jerome? Does he not relate that he was beaten by an angel because he was eagerly pursuing profane learning?[199] Depart from us and take your poets with you." And certain lawyers will fully agree, those whose learning sticks to the glosses rather than to the text, and those who think that one can find nothing in the civil law more elegant than the books of the *authentici*.[200]

Let me respond briefly to these critics. If all the men of Germany should agree with them, we shall gladly leave the country rather than dwell amid so much ignorance or blindness. But even in these regions there are men of learning who care a great deal about the poets and orators and who are not moved by the arguments of their adversaries. For although Marcus Nobilior had his detractors, still he did not yield to the multitude disparaging him; and he was imitated by Scipio Africanus the Elder, who, not content with having loved Ennius, commanded that the poet's statue should be placed on his own tomb and that of his ancestors. So if there is going to be a contest between authorities, I would say that Scipio Africanus and Marcus Nobilior carry greater weight than all the rest of the popular multitude. The citation from Plato given by Cicero can be easily deflected. Hear what Cicero added shortly afterward—these are his own words: "But why are we angry with the poets? Some philosophers, teachers of virtue, may be found who said that pain was the greatest of evils."[201] And immediately he cites a great many examples of philosophers who introduced a pernicious doctrine. Therefore the

63

philosophers ought to have been expelled on the same grounds that Plato excluded the poets.

64   And what should I say about the theologians? What error against faith has not arisen from them? Who introduced the Arian madness, who separated the Greeks from the Church, who seduced the Bohemians, if not the theologians? Once upon a time the Romans drove the whole class of physicians from the city because many crimes were discovered among them, but afterwards, when the guilty had been punished, they received back the innocent. What about the orators? Did not Cicero say that many cities were utterly destroyed because of the eloquence of wicked persons?[202] But just as not all orators, doctors, theologians, and philosophers ought to be rejected because of some bad ones among them, similarly not all poets are to be shunned because of the vices of a few. Otherwise even Plato himself should have been driven from the state which he designed, since he was devoted to tragedy, and his poems, quoted by Macrobius, show that he was himself a poet.[203] Nor would Cicero have remained in that state, since not only was he a very great admirer of the poets, but he also wrote three books of verse *On His Own Times* in the manner of a poet. Boethius' apparent objection deserves to provoke laughter rather than refutation. For who can keep from laughing when it is reported that the art of poetry is being condemned by a poet? Does not Boethius himself wax poetical throughout his writings? When Philosophy herself converses with him, she usually does so in verse and in fictional images. How many stories are there in his works, and how many kinds of meter? Boethius seems to be like the man who used to swear that one should not swear. But we do not blame Boethius, a great philosopher and poet, for what men like these believe; we think he was of an altogether different mind. But it would be a long business to discuss this now.

65   I come now to Jerome, in whose footsteps I should like all living men to follow; we should all be endowed with eloquence and holi-

ness of life like his. There is no need to oppose him, who announced that he had been flogged only after he had ranged over all
the secular studies. I am inclined to think in regard to this business along the lines of the Florentine proverb about family property. They say, "When you have filled up every inch of your
house, *then* remember to live an upright life." Jerome overflows
everywhere with poetic language, nor is there a single line of his
that does not smack of Ciceronian eloquence, even though he denied himself Cicero and the odd pagan book. I would say the
same of the other doctors of the Church, whose smooth tongues,
which would otherwise have been mute, were polished by the poets. No wonder the commander of the Christian army, that invin-
cible orator, the Apostle Paul, used to read attentively the works of
the poets, whose verses are found incorporated in his epistles. For
according to Jerome, what Paul writes to Titus, "Cretans are always liars, wicked beasts, lazy gluttons,"[204] is a verse of the poet
Epimenides. In another place he used a line from Menander: "Evil
conversations corrupt good manners."[205] It is not surprising that a
word-for-word translation does not preserve the meter of the
Latin, since only with difficulty is a line of Homer in the same
tongue made coherent in prose. There is a wide field and rich material for disputation here. An almost infinite number of persons
could be adduced who confirm that profane literature and especially the poets should be read. Indeed, Cyprian, a man distinguished for eloquence and for his martyrdom, was attacked, as
Firmianus relates, because when writing against Demetrianus he
cited the testimony of prophets and apostles, which Demetrianus
said was imaginary and invented, and not rather that of the philosophers and poets, whose authority as a pagan he could not con-
tradict.[206] But what need is there to cite other witnesses beyond
Paul? If someone does not believe Paul, who will he believe? Let
whoever wishes follow his own error; we, along with Paul and
other saints and learned men, far from avoiding the reading of the

poets, shall urge others to embrace such reading lawfully and in moderation.

66   We do not, indeed, lay it down as a principle that all poets should be read and that boys should study them obsessively. There *are* many erotic and vicious things in them, so the mind must not be absorbed in everything they say, just as one should not hear lectures on all the theologians and philosophers. But whenever they recount the words or deeds of outstanding men, then the reader ought to be moved and inspired with his whole mind, and should strive to be as far as possible like them. But when wicked men are referred to, one should avoid imitating them. Listen to Basil, that most holy and knowledgeable man: "We praise the poets," he said, "but not when they relate quarrels, nor when they portray buffoons, lovers, drunkards, or sharp-tongued people, nor when they define happiness as consisting in a rich table and a ribald song; and least of all when they say anything about the gods, especially when they describe them as multiple and discordant." And a little later he says, "The same must also be said of other writers, most of all when they are being read for pleasure." And again, "But then we embrace the orators, particularly when they either extoll virtue or strike down vices." Thus, in reading the poets and other writers, it will be fitting to imitate the bees. For while other animals take only fragrance and color from flowers, bees know also how to suck out the honey. In the same way, those who do not seek merely verbal pleasures can receive some fruit. Moreover, bees do not approach all flowers indiscriminately, nor do they entirely suck dry the ones they land upon, but they leave the rest of the flower well and unharmed after taking what is suited to their work.[207]

67   I cannot refrain from employing the testimony of St. Jerome again, this time to teach how to find a cure in the very place where a wound was inflicted. When he, in a letter written to an orator of the city, had pointed out that Paul had not been ignorant of secu-

lar literature and had used verses of the poets, he immediately added that he had read in Deuteronomy the precept of the Lord, that the head of a captive woman should be shaven, that her eyebrows and all the hair and nails of her body should be removed and that then she might be married. To this he adds on his own: "Is it any wonder that I wish to change pagan learning, because of the charm of its eloquence and the beauty of its limbs, from a handmaid and captive into an Israelite? Is it surprising if I cut off or shave off the parts of it that are dead in idolatry, voluptuousness, error and lust?"[208] This gives you a plan for reading the poets and other authors. For when you shall have received from them whatever is in accordance with the truth, you should pass over all the rest, avoiding the thorns as you gather the roses. You will accept just so much as has been usefully written, and you will decline whatever might be harmful among the rest.

For at the beginning of any discipline, no matter what it may 68 be, you should size it up and direct it towards its object or end. And since we ascend from this life to a better one through virtue, and virtue is much praised by the poets and historians, and even more so by the philosophers, we ought to pay particular attention to their words. For a certain habit of virtue and a familiarity with it, instilled in the minds and youthful souls of boys, has no little usefulness, since whatever is learned at this tender age tends to stick strongly, indeed to be almost impossible to remove.[209] For this reason Horace says:

> An earthen pot, once it has been permeated [with a liquid],
> will preserve the odor for a long time.[210]

Thus a twofold advantage will accrue to you from reading ancient and modern authors who have written with practical wisdom. Through zeal for virtue you will make your life better, and you will acquire the art of grammar and skill in the use of the best and most elegant words, as well as a great store of maxims.

69   But receive this further instruction from us and learn what authors you should read while you are a boy. These are the poets, historians, philosophers, and orators. For we reserve to another time of life the theologians, although some of the latter who also fall into the category of philosophers might be given a boy without danger, as we shall afterwards relate. For there is nothing which philosophy passes over as unknown. Let the judgement of your teacher assist you in reading the poets who will be entrusted to you. Among the epic poets your teacher shall prefer Vergil above all, whose eloquence, whose glory, is so great that it can be neither augmented by praise nor diminished by censure. In him the careful reader will discover the different kinds of style, which are thought to be four: brief, full, dry, and florid.[211] Lucan, a distinguished author of history, and Statius, who is rather polished, should not be overlooked. Ovid is always refined and delightful, but in many places too wanton; yet one should by no means turn one's back on his most famous work, to which he gave the name *Metamorphoses*, for the sake of the knowledge of myths he imparts, which is of no small profit to learn. The others who write in heroic verse are far inferior to these and ought to be called rhymsters rather than poets. In my judgment Claudian and the author of the *Argonauticon*[212] are by no means to be despised.

70   Today there are only three satirists whom we have not lost: Horace, Juvenal, and Persius. Martial also may seem a satirist, but his poetry does not observe the laws of satire. Horace, a little younger than Vergil, was a man of much learning; he is always useful whether you read his *Odes*, his *Art of Poetry*, his *Satires*, or his *Epistles*. Still, there are certain things in him which I would not have read or explained to you while you are a boy. Juvenal, a poet of high genius, has said many things with excessive license, yet in some satires he shows himself so religious that he might seem second to none of the teachers of our faith. Persius is too obscure but

is useful. Martial is pernicious. Although flowery and ornate, he is nevertheless so thick with thorns that you may not pick his roses without being pricked. All the writers of elegies should be withheld from a boy. Tibullus, Propertius, Catullus, and the bits of Sappho that we have in translation are too soft and effeminate. Their writings are almost all about love and they are continually bemoaning their lost loves. So put them aside or let them be reserved for a more robust time of life.

The writers of comedy can contribute much to eloquence, since ⁷¹ they cover all types of person and dispositions. Of these we have only two, Plautus and Terence. The writers of tragedy are also very useful for boys, but besides Seneca, the grandson of the great Seneca,[213] we have no Latin tragedian except Gregorio Correr of Venice, who, when I was a youth, turned into a tragedy the story of Tereus as found in Ovid.[214] When gravity and elegance are called for in your speech, you will find the former in tragedy and the latter in comedy. But your teacher ought to be careful lest he seem to be advocating something vicious while he reads comedies and tragedies to you. But he should bid you weigh and consider the characters who speak and the passions which follow upon those speeches.

There is great mob of orators whom one could read, but Cicero ⁷² is the most brilliant of them all and sufficiently pleasant and clear to beginners. He can be not only profitable but also lovable, and I think that his books *On Duties* are not only useful but even necessary for you. Ambrose also wrote, in imitation of Cicero, a work *On Duties* which is not to be despised. I should think it highly suitable to read it together with Cicero's book, so that anything unorthodox in Cicero may be set straight by Ambrose. The works of Lactantius are highly polished, there is nothing rough in Jerome, the books of Augustine are faultless, and you can make use of Gregory with no small advantage. In our day the works of Leonardo Bruni, Guarino of Verona, Poggio Bracciolini, and Ambrogio Traversari, the Camaldolensian monk, are nicely written and worth reading.

73   Boys ought to read historians, too, like Livy and Sallust, although they will need to be older to understand them. Then we have Justin and Quintus Curtius and Arrian, whom Pier Paolo Vergerio translated, whose writings contain truth, not fables. The deeds of Alexander should be perused. To these writers Valerius Maximus, the historian and philosopher, makes a not unworthy addition. One should not put Suetonius in a boy's hands. Stories from Genesis, the Books of Kings, the Book of Maccabees, Judith, Esdras, Esther, the Gospels, and the Acts of the Apostles are also read with great profit. For, as Cicero says, "history is the witness of the times, the light of truth, the teacher of life, the messenger of antiquity."[215] It is therefore advantageous to know a great deal of history and to train yourself in it, so that by following the example of others you may know how to seek what is useful and to avoid what is harmful. Still, we do not want to involve you in superfluous work, and it is sufficient to have learned the histories repeated or recorded by famous authors. But if my authority is worth anything, I would absolutely forbid the histories of the Bohemians or the Hungarians and similar accounts to be put into a boy's hands. For they are written by ignorant people, and contain much silliness, many lies, no maxims, and no elegance of style. What Pliny says, that "no book is so bad that nothing useful can be taken from it,"[216] may seem to justify giving him anything at all to read, but the statement refers not to boys but to men who are already educated. Unless boys are steeped from the beginning in the best books, their minds will be ruined and they will not be able to acquire good judgement.

74   You should now think that enough has been said concerning the second part of grammar — once, that is, we have observed that these authors, in our judgement, ought not to be ingested at the

same time, nor must you necessarily study all of them, and you should take every precaution to prevent the great labor involved from making you hate literature.

It was stated earlier that the third part of grammar consists of 75 orthography, i.e., the art of writing well. Perhaps it will seem a very trifling matter if I should also give you rules concerning this part, because it may seem silly for a king to be engaged in writing letters and because gentlemen usually take little care to write well and quickly. But it is not out of place to teach even this part of grammar to a royal youth, for it sheds no small light on the comprehension and understanding of the authors. Indeed it is related that many of the old Caesars were highly skilled penmen. Pope Nicholas V, who at this moment presides over the Church of Rome, writes an elegant hand; and his predecessor, Eugene IV, has a similar skill; nor would anyone criticize the script of your glorious uncle, Emperor Frederick. Although a ruler must write only rarely, still, when he does write, he should take care that he does not appear to be drawing flysmears rather than pearls. It dims somewhat the glory of Alfonso, a very great and otherwise very excellent king,[217] that one does not know, when he adds his own name to the letters written from his curia, whether he is drawing snakes or letters. That you may not share in this defect, pay attention to our advice respecting orthography. "The labor is small," as Vergil says, "but not the glory."[218]

Orthography we divide into two parts: writing clearly and writing correctly.[219] In the first part, one must be sure to form the letters with their proper characteristics, neither too long nor too thick, letting the round, square, extended and curly shapes keep their proper form. And here, too, there are two ways of doing things, one modern and one ancient.[220] The form of ancient letters is more legible, pure, and closer to the Greeks from whom it takes its origin. Whatever style a boy wishes to follow, he needs to be given a beautiful and perfectly correct model of it, for the best models should always be presented for imitation. If we cannot attain the best, they will at least accomplish this, that we are not despised along with the worst. It would be useful also to make sure that the verses chosen for writing samples contain no unprofitable thoughts or barbarous words. Rather they should contain some noble admonition, selected from illustrious poets and from famous authors, so that in this way a boy may learn to philosophize and to write as if he were playing a game.

77   In the second part, regarding correct writing, numerous rules are taught, and one must learn the vowels, consonants, mutes, liquids, and double letters must be known. Simple words should be considered according to their characteristic elements so that an analogous study of compounds may be made. But this also allows many an exception, and there are many changes not just of letters but of whole syllables when it comes both to inflections and compound words. But we learn more by use than by rule the letters in which simple words should be written: in this matter the reading of the poets is of the greatest assistance, for the meters, by showing whether the syllables are long or short, prescribe whether letters should be doubled or removed. By this argument one clearly learns that *oppidum* should be spelt with the *p* doubled, because poets have made its first syllable long, as in that verse of Vergil:

tot congesta manu praeruptis oppida saxis.[221]
So many towns cut by hand from the sheer rock.

For the first syllable would have been short if he had retained only one *p*, as *oportet*. But although *opportunus* is derived from *oportet*, it requires the *p* doubled, as the usage of the learned indicates.

78   The rules governing changes of letters mostly have to do with compound words, which are usually formed with prepositions. It is therefore expedient to know how the preposition *ad* enters into composition with different words. Sometimes the *d* is changed into the letter following it, with which the locution joined to it be-

gins, as *curro, accurro; fero, affero; gero, aggero; ludo, alludo; nuntio, annuntio; pono, appono; rideo, arrideo; surgo, assurgo; tollo, attollo;* etc.[222] As regards other compounds which are made with words beginning with the same letters as those which are compounded with the preposition *ad,* sometimes the *d* is lost, as *aperio* from *ad* and *pario,* and *agnitus, aspectus,* and *ascendo,* and *asto, ascribo,* and *astruo,* and this rule must always be observed when *ad* is united to a locution beginning with *gn, sp,* or *sc,* or any consonant following *s.* Otherwise *d* will remain unchanged, as *adhibeo, adhaereo, advoco, adquiro* — not *acquiro* as many would have it, though in this case, perhaps, custom has by now vanquished logic.[223] There are those who write *adsum* and those who write *assum,* when *ad* and *sum* are compounded, and there are learned men on both sides of this issue, so custom seems to prevail in both cases. In Quintilian's view both *absum* and *apsum, obtimus* and *optimus* can be written, because *p* and *b* have a cognate sound.[224] The perfect of the verb *absum* is found written *affui* and *abfui,* though the latter seems more logical. The preposition *ab* does not ordinarily lose *b* when linked to any word whatsoever, as *abdo, abicio, abero,* and *abripio.* If the *b* were changed into the following consonant, the compound would seem to be formed from *ad* rather than *ab.* Still it is customary to write *amitto,* not *abmitto,* and *absporto* is formed with an interposed *s,* although it is from *ab* and *porto.*

The writer should know that no consonant can be doubled if a 79 consonant precedes or follows it,[225] unless it is *l* or *f* before *r,* which follows or precedes, as *effluo, effringo,* and *suffragor.* We do not say *trassumo,* but *transumo,* although it is composed of *trans* and *sumo.* Yet three consonants can occur together if none is to be doubled, like *obscenus, sanctio,* and *sextus,* for *x* has the force of two consonants, *cs* or *gs.* When the preposition *ex* is united to words beginning with *s,* it does not allow *s* to occur simultaneously, but it throws it out, as in *exurgo, exigo, exanguis,* and *exectus.* But if it is compounded with a word beginning with *f*, the *x* will change to *f*, as *effugio*, *effero*, and *effringo*. Otherwise it neither changes nor is changed, as *excurro*, *exquiro*, *expello*, *extendo*, and *exlex*. No other word beginning with *l* is found formed with *ex*. But the preposition *e* is added to many words to which *ex* cannot be prefixed, as though the first letter of the word were *d*, as *educo*, or consonantal *u*, as *evoco*, *evacuo*, and *eveho*, or consonantal *i*, as *eiicio*, or *n*, as *enitor*, or *m*, as *emineo*, or *r*, as *eruo*.

80   There is no way that such consonants may be doubled, although *eiicio* is written with double *i* because the second *i* is a vowel, not a consonant; and the word *eiicio* preserves the double *i* throughout its entire declension, one the consonant and the other the vowel, except when the letter *e* follows, as *eieci*. In prose, too, any word coming from *iacio* ought to be written with double *i*, as *eiicio*, *obiicio*, *reiicio*, and *abiicio*. But in verse it must be noticed whether the first syllable is long or short. If it is long, the *i* is doubled; if short, it will be simple. Each usage of these words is found in Vergil:

> *Tityre, pascentes a flumine reice capellas,*[226]
> Tityrus, drive from the river the grazing she-goats,

nor is there a proceleusmatic in the fifth foot as it has seemed to some. Ovid has:

> *quid mihi livor edax ignavos obicis annos;*[227]
> Why does gnawing spite burden my torpid years?

and Statius:

> *pectoraque invisis obicit fumantia muris;*[228]
> He leans their smoking bodies against the hated walls

and again:

> *frondibus instantis abicit monstratque cruorem;*[229]

he abandons them as they press into the foliage and displays
the gore.

and elsewhere:

abicit; attonitae tectorum e culmine summo.[230]
he throws away [the olive branch], and thunderstruck from
the rooftops.

Quintilian, too, thinks that *coniicio* should be written with double
i.[231] *In* and *con*, when compounded with words beginning with *l, r,*
or *m*, change the *n* into the following letter and double it, as *ludo,
illudo, colludo; ruo, irruo, corruo; muto, immuto, commuto;* and *mitto,
immitto, committo.*[232] But the preposition *con* is inseparable and is
found only in compounds; and when it is united to a word which
begins with a vowel or aspirate, it loses the *n*, as in *coerceo, cohaereo,*
and *cohortor.* The word *comedo* is deceptive on this point, compounded as it is from *con* and *edo*, where for the sake of euphony *n*
is not dropped but changes into *m.*[233]

Where *sub* and *ob* have been united to words beginning with *r,*   81
p, c, g, f, or *m*, they usually have the *b* changed to the following
consonant and doubled, as *succurro, occurro, succido, occido, succumbo,
occumbo, succino, occino, sufficio, officio, suggero, summitto, ommutesco,
suppono, oppono,* and *surripio.* Yet there are these exceptions: *aufero*
and *aufugio*, in which *b* is changed to *u*; likewise *obrogo, obrado,* and
obrodo, in which *b* remains unchanged. If *sub* is united to the word
quatio, b is changed to *c* and the word is spelled *sucquatio.* Likewise
we must write *omitto*, not *ommitto* or *obmitto.*[234] *Operio* and its passive *operior* are happy with only a single *p*, while the deponent
opperior requires the double *p*. *Opinor, opinio, opitulor,* and *opulentus*
take a single *p*. Sometimes *ob*, when *r* follows, remains unchanged
for the sake of euphony, as in *obruo, obrepo,* and *obripio. Obscurus*
also, formed from *ob* and *curo*, does not change its *b* but takes an *s*
because of the consonant. This happens also in *obscoenus,* a com-

pound of *ob* and *coenus*. But if *ob* and *sub* are compounded with words other than the aforesaid words, they preserve the *b* unchanged, as in *subdo* and *obdo*.

82 The inseparable prepositions in *dis-* and *di-* are found in compounds only. *Dis-* can be compounded with words in *c, p, s, t,* consonental *i,* or *s,* as *discerno* from *dis-* and *cerno, dispono, distraho, disiungo,* and *dissuo,* and is preserved without any change of *s;* in the word *diffundo, s* is changed to *f* and doubled, as in *differo* and *diffido; dimminuo* also is from *dis-* and *minuo,* where *s* is changed to *m* and doubled.[235] Nor can *di-* be compounded with words beginning in this way, except with *minuo,* and then it ought to be written with simple *m,* as in *diminuo. Di-* is more frequently united with other words than *dis-,* as in *diduco, diluo, dinumero, diruo, digladior,* and *diripio.*

83 The preposition *trans* compounded with words beginning with *d, n* or consonantal *i* loses *n* and *s,* as in *traduco, trano,* and *traiicio.* It is also found unchanged, as *transmigro* and *transduco,* which appear not to be compounds.[236] The letter *n* cannot be placed before *b, m,* or *p,* whether the locution is simple or compound, as in *summa* with double *m, rombus, Pompeius, communis, immunis, combibo, imbibo, computo,* and *imputo.* Also, in compounds separated because of the figure of speech called *tmesis,* as in *im quam prudens* and *im quam potens,* the usage of the learned has it that *m* is put in place of *n,* although it might seem right for it to revert to the preposition in keeping with its nature, since it does not change while it is separated, even if the word following should begin with the abovementioned letters, as in *in bivio, in pontificio,* and *in magistratu.* On the contrary it happens that *f, c, d, q,* and *t,* both in simple and compound words, do not allow *m* to precede them immediately, as *tonsus, linquo, cancer, mendax, centum, anfractus, quemcunque, quicunque, tantundem,* and *identidem.* Also in Greek words which are formed with *ph,* the same principle is to be observed, but the more

learned prefer *Pamphilus* and *nympha* to be written with *m*, but pronounced as *n*.

When the preposition *circum* is compounded with a word beginning with a vowel, it preserves the *m* unchanged, so that *circumeo* is so written, but pronounced *circueo*. The preposition *cum* ought to be written *c, u, m*, but if it is an adverb of time, in Quintilian's opinion, it should be written *qu, u, o, m*;[237] hence we write *quondam*, not *condam*. It was an ancient custom also to write *Caium* and *Cnaeum*, but to pronounce *Gaium, Gnaeum*; and there are those who today still observe this—learned men and lovers of antiquity. Thus it happens that letters do not always represent the true sound of the word, but sometimes one letter exhibits the sound of another, as when we write *amantium* and *amentium* with a *t* and pronounce the sound as *c*. Yet *litium* and *vitium*, the genitive plurals of *litus* and *vites*, do not change the sound lest they should he considered *licium*, *licii*, and *vicium*, *vicii*. Inverted C according to Quintilian signifies a woman, *Gaia*, as C signifies a man, *Gaius*.[238] Likewise Quintilian thought we should write *quicquid*, Vittorino[239] *quidquid*, as if it were divided and *quid* repeated, which seemed the preferable spelling to Gasparino Barzizza.[240] But the learned write *idcirco*, not *iccirco*, because it is identical to *circa id*. But *quicquam* is written, not *quidquam*, and hence *nequicquam*. It happens frequently also that *c* is changed into *g* as in number words if preceded by *n*, as in *quadringenti* and *quingenti*, but if *n* does not precede, *c* stays unchanged, as in *ducenti* and *trecenti*.

Sometimes letters are inserted to make them sound better, as *c* in *sicubi* from *si* and *ubi*; *t*, as *identidem* from *idem* and *idem*; *p*, as in *emptum*, which comes from *emo*; *b*, as in *ambio* from the imperfect particle *am* and *eo*; *s*, as in *obscurus* from *ob* and *cura*; *l*, as in *obliquus* from *ob* and *equus*; *r*, as in *dirimo* from *di* and *emo*; consonantal *u*, as in *bovis* from the nominative *bos*. The letter *k*, as Quintilian says, is useless since *c* occurs in its place in all words.[241] Still it has its uses,

84

85

as in *Karolus* and *kalendae*, which are written with *k*, not *c*. And since orthography is a great servant of custom, we should not abandon it, since it is becoming to have custom, which is established by good and learned men, as our teacher for speech and for life as well as for writing. The interrogative adverb *cur* can be written *c* or *qu*, but when it has *qu* it requires double *u*, as *quur*. Greek words beginning with *r* ought to be aspirated, as *rhetor*, *Rhodus*, and *Rhadamanthys*. *Rhenus* and *Rhodanus* are also aspirated, for in ancient times both the Germans and the Gauls used Greek letters, and these rivers were named by the Greeks.

86   But since we have mentioned aspiration, let us continue this part a little further. All words which come from *hypo* must be aspirated at the beginning and must be written with *y* and one *p*, as *hyperbole*, *hyperboreus*, *hypotheca*, and *hypocrita*. Similarly, words which come from *hippos* are aspirated, but are written in Latin with *i* and double *p*, as *hippocentaurus*, *Hippomenes*, *Hippodamia*, and *Hippolytus*. But if *hippos* is the suffix of a compound, it loses the aspiration (the rest keep it), as in *Philippus*, which is from *philos*, i.e., "lover," and *hippos*, "horse," meaning "lover of horses."²⁴² But *hypo* is a Greek preposition which in Latin signifies *sub*. Among the Latins no consonant is aspirated, though Servius makes an exception of *pulcher*. The ancients also aspirated *sepulchrum*. *Inchoo* and *incoo* are found aspirated and unaspirated, because Papias thinks the word comes from the Greek while Servius contends that it is Latin. Logic urges that we write *mihi*, not *michi* and *nihil*, not *nichil*, since *c* is nowhere aspirated except in *pulcher* and, as some will have it, *inchoo*, *orcho*, and *sepulchro*.²⁴³ Besides, there are four consonants which are according to our custom aspirated in Greek words: *c*, *p*, *r*, and *t*, as *Chremes*, *philosophus*, *rhetor*, and *Thraso*.²⁴⁴ All words which come from *archos* are aspirated, as *archidiaconus*, *archipresbyter*, *architriclinus*, *archiepiscopus*, *patriarcha*, and *monarcha*; similarly, whatever words come from *cheiros*, as *chiromantia*, *chiromanticus*, *chirotheca*, and *chirurgia*, which have been adapted for our use from Greek

words. Those in which *f* seems to sound ought to be written with *ph*, as *Phoebus, Phaethon, Pharus,* and *Orpheus,* except *filius, fero,* and *fama,* which, although they have slipped in from Greek, are nevertheless written with *f.* For *filius* is said to be from *philos,* i.e., "lover," or *philis,* which is "love." *Fero* is Greek and in the first person differs in no respect from the Greek; one says *fero, feris, feri.* And *fama* is from *phemi,* a Greek verb which means "I say," because *fama* arises from the sayings or speeches of many men. Whatever comes from *aether,* as in *aethra* and *aethereus,* or from *ethos,* as in *ethica* and *ethicus,* or from *orthos,* as *orthographia* and *orthographus,* or from *theca,* as *bibliotheca* and *chirotheca,* or from *theos,* as *theologus* and *theologia,* or from *thesis,* as *synthesis* and *hypothesis,* ought to be written with a *t* and aspirated.

This is not the case with words that come from *protos, anti, kata,* and *meta,* such as *protomartyr, protonotarius, antithesis, anticato, catalogus, metamorphoseos,* and *metaplasmus. Y* [Greek *i*] never changes into a consonant, and therefore those who write *Yhesus, Yherusalem,* and *Yheremias* are unintelligent, for although these words are foreign they still require our *i,* not a foreign one. No logic permits *p* to be placed between *m* and *n,* and *columpna, tirampnus,* and *contempno* are thus incorrectly written by many. We must write *autumnus,* not *auptumnus* or *autumpnus;* it doesn't need a *p;* likewise with *somnium, somnus, alumnus, amnis, omnis, solemnis,* and *scamnum.* In Vergil, *Mnestheus* strangely preserves *m* before *n.* But *contempsi, contemptum, prompsi, promptum, dempsi, demptum, carpsi, carptum, emi, emptum,* and *campsi, camptum* preserve the *p. Pessimus* ought to be written with double *s,* not *x;* no words except *maximus* and *proximus* may end with the superlative in -*ximus.* Moral or imitative verbs can be written with double *s,* as in *matrisso, patrisso,* and *fratrisso,* or with *z,* as in *matrizo, patrizo,* and *fratrizo.* The word *nitor, niteris,* when it refers to bodily effort, forms its perfect *nixus* with *x,* but when it refers to the soul, *nisus* with only one *s.*

87

88   But I have written enough for you regarding the general rules of orthography. What remains for you to learn about the spelling of individual words the experience of reading the authors repeatedly will supply.

89   When studying grammar, it is usual to point out also the rules of rhetoric. For when one reads the orators and poets, the power of true rhetoric is disclosed. There one finds figures of speech, embellishments, and maxims; men are praised and blamed; judgements and arguments are to hand. Every part of rhetoric is thoroughly cultivated by the poets and historians. But in them you find the practice of rhetoric; its theory is taught by the orators, especially Cicero and Quintilian. There is also the *Rhetoric* of Aristotle, translated into Latin in our time,[245] which is quite useful. You can safely make use of these authors; the others are crude and can seem to unteach rather than teach. For example, there is the fellow who recently published a new *Rhetoric* at Vienna which has much true and useful material from Cicero mixed into it, yet thanks to the corrupt words and examples it contains he has made it so that its teachings are neither true nor useful.[246] He and his like must be avoided; one should drink from the spring, not downstream. You should, then, learn several precepts of the art of rhetoric which have been taken from tested and famous authors. You should know what the duty of an orator is, and you should learn how properly to discover, arrange, embellish, memorize, and deliver the parts of an oration.[247] But since our desire is that you be a perfect king more than a good orator, we do not require of you the eloquence of a Cicero or a Demosthenes. Yet we would desire this: that you be elegant in your speech, for this will bring you great distinction and advantage. But since there are many things which a king is under the pressure of necessity to learn, one thing should not hinder the other; a moderate eloquence will be sufficient for a king.

But since in presenting the precepts of rhetoric it is customary 90
not to pass over dialectic in silence — for rhetoric and dialectic are
in a certain sense interchangeable, as both alike try not only to
devise and present arguments, but also to defend and accuse — it
will not be irrelevant for a royal youth to be initiated into the rules
of dialectic. He should be so taught that after he has grasped the
divisions of logic, which Cicero defined as "a careful pattern of discussion,"[248] he may learn how to define, to distribute, and to com-
bine; and he should be aware that the technique of inference can
be set out in three different ways, since a disputation proceeds either with true and necessary arguments, or with ones that are
merely probable, or with ones that are patently false. In this subject, however, I would say that certain Viennese persons are not
worthy of imitation, as they spend too much time in sophistical
and hair-splitting arguments, so that for them the study of logic
comes to an end in death rather than in any useful outcome. That
is why in his books *On Duties*, Cicero does not approve of Gaius
Sulpicius or Sextus Pompey, who devoted too much care and
effort to geometry and not enough to dialectic or civil law. For although arts of this sort engage in investigation of truth, it is contrary to duty to be drawn away from attending to our affairs by
studying them, since all the glory of virtue, as he says, consists
in action.[249] Superfluous imitation should be avoided in every art,
for even though such imitation seems harmless, it still requires
vain effort and takes us away from useful business. Such was the
man who, as Quintilian relates, with continuous success shot
grains of chick-peas through a needle from a distance; after Alexander had seen him, he is said to have given the man a peck of this
legume, which was certainly a worthy reward for such an achievement.[250]

It may be asked whether the art of music should also be taught 91
to a young prince, since it would seem to contribute little or noth-

ing to the governance of a state. Nero and Augustus were bitterly
criticized for devoting themselves too enthusiastically to music;
Augustus, having been rebuked, gave it up, while Nero redoubled
his devotion to the art.[251] When Philip of Macedon wished to correct a certain harpist in the midst of a banquet, and to discuss
with him the art of plucking the strings, the harpist said: "May
the gods protect you from this evil, O king: that you should
have a better grasp of this art than I."[252] On the other hand,
Themistocles, the Greek leader, was considered uneducated for
having refused the lyre at a banquet.[253] Socrates, the fountain of
philosophers, was not afraid to learn the lyre in his old age,[254] for
it was proverbial that the ignorant kept their distance from the
Muses and the Greeks.[255] The army of the Lacedaemonians usually won when it had been drilled using musical measures.[256]
Gracchus, the chief orator of his day, ordered music to sound as
he was addressing the people.[257] And was not David skilled in this
art, was he not accustomed to use the harmonious harp to relieve
the sufferings of Saul?[258] There is no doubt that Lycurgus too
praised this art, despite his having given extremely harsh laws to
the Spartans.[259] Hence it was a custom among the ancients that
the praises of heroes and gods should be chanted at their banquets
to the sound of the zither. And what about Vergil's Ioppas? Does
he not sing of the wandering moon and the labors of the sun, and
the rest, by which our illustrious author confirms that music is
linked to knowledge of the divine?[260]

92   But what shall we say amid so great a variety of views, since
some would urge training in this art and others oppose it? It is
surely not an art to be despised, nor should its use be censured,
but the excessive practice of it should be barred. Therefore a moderate knowledge of this art ought not to be shunned, if good instructors may be found. For musical harmony which is neither im-
moderate nor sensuous greatly refreshes the spirit and cheers the
mind for enduring hardship. It was thus a custom for the Pythago-

reans to banish whatever sadness they might have by the sweet playing of the lyre when they retired at night and when they rose in the morning.[261] Some claim that Pythagoras was the inventor of this art, others Moses, others Tubal.[262] But I am surprised at this opinion of the pagans concerning Pythagoras, since all the poets declare that Orpheus, who preceded Pythagoras not by years but by centuries, was highly skilled in music.

Boys in their tender years should also be introduced to geome- 93 try, for this study sharpens the intellect and makes the mind quick to understand.[263] This implies a knowledge of arithmetic, too, since geometry is divided into numbers and shapes, and no one, certainly, denies that kings need a knowledge of arithmetic. So it is not unbecoming for a young prince to pursue the study of both geometry and arithmetic at the same time. If anyone thinks that geometry should be despised, he can be defeated by the testimony of the Syracusans who, when Marcus Marcellus was bringing his siege engines up against the city, were able to prolong the siege by the genius of Archimedes alone and his powers of geometry.[264] Besides, there is much to be learned in it and it makes us extremely cautious, since very often this art does not allow what it seems that logic should allow. For who would not believe someone who asserted the following: when the boundary lines around places measure the same, all figures that can be inscribed within those bounding lines are necessarily equal in area. But this is fallacious, since it makes a great difference what figure the boundary lines form, and historians, as Quintilian says, who have thought that the dimensions of islands are adequately reckoned by the distance traversed in sailing round them have been justly censured by geometricians. For the nearer to perfection any figure is, the greater is its capacity; and if, therefore, the boundary line forms a circle, it embraces a larger area than if it forms a square of equal circumference. Again, squares contain more area than triangles, and triangles of equal sides contain more area than those of unequal sides.

But in hills and valleys it is evident even to the uninitiated that there is more [surface area in the] ground than there is sky, and it is known that the measure of an acre is two hundred and forty feet in length and half that in width, and it is easy to calculate what its circumference is and how much ground it contains. But one hundred and eighty feet on each side has the same perimeter but encloses a much larger area.[265] Although it is useful and delightful to grasp such arts, I should nevertheless not recommend too much expenditure of time upon them, because even if they are advantageous for those who survey the subject, they can nevertheless be harmful for those who get involved in them for too long.

94   Nor should a moderate study of astronomy, a study which explains the heavens and discloses the secrets of the heavenly bodies to mortals, be denied a young prince. A knowledge of this subject has often been a helpful and seemly thing for great leaders. At Athens when the soldiers, terrified by the darkening of the sun, were planning flight, Pericles, by explaining the cause of the phenomenon, kept control of the army and emerged as the victor. When the spirits of the soldiers in the army of Lucius Paulus grew terrified because of an eclipse of the moon, as though a divine omen had been delivered, Gallus Sulpicius, by pointing out the natural explanation, put their minds at rest. And Dion of Syracuse was not frightened by a similar event when he came to destroy the tyrant Dionysius, because he had been a disciple of Plato and skilled in astronomy. And if Nicias had known this in Sicily, he would not have betrayed that most splendid Athenian army through being disturbed by the same fear.[266] Therefore a boy should also be immersed in this branch of knowledge, without which the poets cannot be completely understood.[267] But we must always take care, when taking on one art, not to neglect the others, nor should our attachment to natural science and contemplative studies lead us to put aside the study of morality and distract us from the conduct of our affairs.

Someone may perhaps inquire how these things are to be 95
learned and whether they can be taught and understood at the
same time. Some will deny that this is possible because the mind
is confused and wearied by so many studies tending in different
directions. But these people do not sufficiently appreciate how
great is the power of the human mind, which is so busy, so active
and so universally curious that it is impossible for it to limit its activity to one thing only; rather it expends its whole power on
many subjects, not only in the course of a single day, but even in a
single moment of time. Variety itself refreshes and renews the
spirit. Who would not grow dull if he had to endure a single
teacher of a single art for a whole day? The spirit will be refreshed
by change as the stomach is invigorated by a moderate variety of
food. Farmers cultivate at the same time their fields, their vine-
yards, their olive trees, and their groves; they care for their mead-
ows, their herds, their birds, and their bees.[268] So why may not
boys, whose dispositions are much more docile than those of
young men, pursue various disciplines, I do not say at the same
moment, but during the same period of time? Those who govern
you while you are a boy, then, should take care that throughout
the day you listen to different teachers, that you devote yourself
now to grammar, now to dialectic, and now to some other branch
of knowledge, and they will not refuse you proper times for play
and physical exercises.

But although the intellect is greatly enlightened by studies of 96
this kind, nevertheless it is not immediately evident what counts
as honorable, what disgraceful, and what just; what is to be chosen
and what avoided. The marks of virtue have not been set forth
completely in the poets, orators, and historians; they are merely
adumbrated. From these studies you must rise higher and give
yourself passionately to real philosophy, a study which we mentioned at the beginning [of this treatise]. But here perhaps some
member of your household will say: "What are you about,

Aeneas? The boy is already sweating over the arts, seven of which you have mentioned so far; is he now to take up philosophy? Why are we returning to this subject?" But a man like this does not know what the name of philosopher means. The inventor of the name, it is agreed, was Pythagoras. For in former times, when good and learned men used to be called wise, fleeing pride, he wanted to be called a philosopher, that is, a lover of wisdom, not a wise man.[269] Hence philosophy can be translated as "love of wisdom." Wisdom embraces not only the seven arts mentioned above but professes the knowledge of all things human and divine and of the causes by which these things are sustained and held together. Therefore one will not be called a philosopher because he pursues the seven arts; nevertheless he will have acquired a part of philosophy. Philosophers at the beginning paid attention only to natural causes, following Thales, the Milesian, who is said to have been the first to speculate about them. Then came Socrates who called moral philosophy down from the heavens,[270] and as a result philosophy was divided into two parts: one called "natural," the other "moral." But with the arrival of the divine Plato's genius, it was decided to add a third part, called "rational."[271]

97　　But thus far we have said little about the moral conduct which is to be learned from philosophy. That is why we once again send the boy back to moral philosophy at the conclusion of our book — but not at the conclusion of his studies. Moral philosophy will point out with demonstrative arguments the worship to be paid to the Divine Majesty, the behavior we should exhibit towards our parents, our elders, foreigners, officials, soldiers, friends, wives, citizens, peasants, and slaves. Moral philosophy will teach you, illustrious king, to despise avarice, greediness for money, for which, as Sallust says, no wise man ever lusts. Moral philosophy will advise you to behave modestly towards women, to hold your children and your relatives dear, to treat servants without cruelty, to respect your elders, to obey the laws, to control anger, to despise pleasures, to pity the oppressed, to succor the needy, to confer rewards on those who deserve them, to render to everyone his due, and to punish the guilty. And what is most important of all, moral philosophy will not allow you to overflow with joy at the favorable turns of fortune or to be cast down with sadness at adverse misfortunes,[272] and it will offer you a way to live rightly and rule your subjects usefully. All this should certainly not to be withheld from a boy, so long as the books chosen for his instruction are pleasant and clear, elegant and polished, as we have indicated above with respect to numerous titles. To those may be added Cicero's *Tusculan Disputations, On Old Age, On Friendship*, and whatever else he has written on morals. Seneca is to be accepted as useful, as also Pliny in his letters and Boethius in his *Consolation of Philosophy*. I should not deny that, apart from these, there exist a great many books by learned men which can safely be given to boys. But I insist that the teacher should exercise good judgement; he should ascertain that such books are polished, well-written and authoritative.

But since that part of philosophy which is called "ethics" leaves 98 no period of human life untouched, but governs youths, mature men, and the elderly, we believe that for the present we have pointed out sufficiently how much should be taught to a boy and from what sources his readings should be taken. We shall have to speak in a still more energetic style in other books as the periods of your life require, if God, the Creator of the world and the Author of the soul, shall prolong our life — unless we shall judge it more modest to be silent rather than speak further after you have read (at our bidding) so many distinguished authors. Meanwhile, endeavor to practice and learn what you have been taught to do as a boy, so that you may show your great zeal for the other parts of this small work. Farewell.

BATTISTA GUARINO TO MAFFEO GAMBARA OF BRESCIA, HIS NOBLE YOUNG STUDENT: A PROGRAM OF TEACHING AND LEARNING

My dearest Maffeo: even though the refinement of your character 1
and ability is such that you have already spontaneously come to
the conclusion that true nobility comes not from wealth or from
the death-masks of one's ancestors[1] (which fortune has bestowed
upon you with a generous hand), but in virtue, I have nevertheless
learned that, from reading the satire of our Juvenal (who sums up
the matter so brilliantly),[2] you have recently fixed this view in your
mind to such an extent that you have come to be still more eager
and fervent in devoting yourself to the humanities. I have accordingly considered it my duty as a good teacher to set out some
method and course of studies through which you might fulfill your
desire with the greatest ease and, as if spurring on a horse that is
already galloping freely,[3] urge yourself on with redoubled zeal. I
have therefore dedicated this booklet to you. From it you may
learn the function and methods both of the teacher who educates
youths in Greek and Latin and of the pupils themselves who are
learning these subjects. If you think any part of it is irrelevant to
you, please believe that my intention was to bestow this little commentary on learning and teaching not so much upon you as upon
other youths under your name; take only what you feel you need.

I would not hesitate to affirm that those who have been taught 2
using a method of this kind are to be counted among the most
learned of men of all time, for I have brought together the meth-

ods most conducive to teaching and learning, following not only my own judgment, which can hardly be of great weight given my youth, but also that of the most learned men, especially my esteemed father, who, as you know, has been a practicing teacher for a very long time. So as you read this, please consider the speaker to be my father, not me, and be assured that nothing has been written here which has not been tested by long practice. But I don't want you to think that I am giving the work false praise: look into the matter yourself and you will recognize, I hope, that these precepts, applied diligently, are true.

3   Nevertheless before we come to the precepts of study and teaching, it is highly relevant to our undertaking to advise young people themselves, first, to acquire spontaneously a real desire to learn—something a teacher can't give them from the outside—and act like a case of dropsy, for whom, as Ovid says,

the more water it drinks, the more it thirsts for.[4]

And so the more knowledge they acquire each day, the more knowledge they are stimulated to seize and drink in, as though longing to quench a chronic thirst. Let them always keep in mind the teaching of the Greek Socrates: if you are eager to learn, you will learn much. They will find ready encouragement to acquire that eagerness, as the same Socrates says, if they see how shameful it is that merchants sail far across the seas to increase their wealth, while young people go by land seeking teachers to improve their minds;[5] if they also keep in mind that no possession is more honorable or stable than learning, for beauty and strength, even when not diminished by any disease, are surely laid low in the end by old age, and money more often provides an excuse for sloth than a means for attaining virtue. Though it is far from easy for those placed in great poverty to rise from obscurity,[6] the affluent are ensnared by pleasure with the greatest of ease. When a kingdom of pleasure is at hand, it is difficult for virtue to stand firm. But if, owing to the feebleness of their age, young persons lack the discernment to acknowledge this truth, it will be the duty of their parents to accustom their tender ears to it with winsome words and to deter them from pleasures with threats, so that the zeal [for learning and virtue] they have imbibed from infancy may grow as they get older, and when as adults they shall hear the sermons of Pleasure, they will shrink from them and loathe them like poison, as though the paternal voice were still ringing in their ears.

Next, let them show parental reverence when honoring their teacher, for if they scorn him, they will also necessarily scorn his teaching. Let us not think our ancestors were rash when they deemed that a teacher should stand in the place of a venerated parent; it was their belief that in this way a teacher would instruct his pupils with greater care and good will, and that his pupils would respect his words reverently as though they flowed from paternal affection.[7] So in this matter let them imitate the example of Alexander the Great, who used to declare that he owed no less to his teacher Aristotle than to Philip his father, because from the latter he had only received life, but from the former he had received the good life.[8] Indeed a mind so educated will offer such promise and high hope as to surpass not only everyone's expectations, but even their prayers. For as Sallust says, "when you apply your intellect, it prevails."[9] And it is of capital importance not to hand over beginning pupils to coarse and uneducated teachers. For the pupils of such men as Cicero says, return "dumber by half" than when they left.[10] Not to mention the time they lose: unquestionably the result will be as Timotheus the musician describes: that afterwards [the new teacher] has twice as much work. First, he must make his pupils forget what they have learned, which is really very difficult, for according to the opinion of Horace:

4

a new earthenware jar will preserve for a long time
the fragrance with which it has once been imbued.[11]

Then he has the second task of inculcating better precepts, which is accomplished all the more slowly as they need to waste time and effort obliterating the previous ones.[12]

5   Every effort should be made to prevent boys from being severely and violently beaten as a matter of educational discipline. Such punishment has something slave-like about it, and it often happens that a noble youth becomes so outraged that the beatings make him hate literature before he has even had a taste of it.[13] Add to this the fact that, from fear of being beaten, students do not compose the declamations assigned to them using their own wits, but produce works secretly composed by others. This is a most pernicious, deadly thing. It is a tremendous deception both for teacher and student, for the former acquires false expectations, while the latter pretends to have done something which he does not in fact understand. It will be more honorable and useful either to employ charm and flattery, or (on occasion) to frighten them with the threat of an immediate beating. If the student feels himself secure from beating, this will open wide the door to negligence. If one is dealing with older students who can be stimulated by the desire for honor, they should be reminded how shameful it will be for them to waste their efforts and to appear duller and more slothful than the rest.

6   To make ignorance more shameful for them than learning, it is well to give the boys some companion in study to kindle in them a spirit of emulation. The finest souls are born with a kind of noble envy, which make them ashamed to be overtaken by those engaged in the same kind of activity and to be left behind as though they were weaklings. Hence competition and rivalries between students make them keener.[14] Nevertheless, we do not approve of having a great number of children taught the basics at the same time under the same teacher, for when a teacher wants to satisfy everyone and to give a share of his time to everyone, he will not give complete or extensive attention to anyone. As a result, no one

is neglected, but no one comes home well taught, either. This is our advice in the case of those learning the rudiments of letters; for those who are somewhat more advanced, already able to hear lectures on the poets, historians and orators, it is hardly necessary.[15] The greater the crowd, the more diligently the teacher himself will try to teach, since, as Ovid says, "a listener excites zeal."[16]

In teaching the former [beginning students], however, he 7 should stick to the following order: they should get used to pronouncing the letters and words clearly and easily, but not with excessive precision. For just as mumbling between your teeth and mangling your words is hard to understand, so a forced pronunciation of letters and a drawling pronunciation of syllables is unpleasant and fussy. Secondly, pupils should be given a complete and perfect command of grammar, for just as, in the case of buildings, everything that you build on top necessarily collapses unless strong foundations have been laid, so too in one's plan of study: unless pupils acquire an excellent knowledge of the basics, greater progress will only make them more aware of their weaknesses. Consequently, let boys learn first to decline their nouns and conjugate their verbs; without this, there is no way they will be able to come to an understanding of what comes next. And the teacher should not be content to have taught [the paradigms] once only, but should repeat them over and over, training the boys' memories on them. Like an energetic general he should inspect what they have learned and to what degree. From time to time he should himself make some mistakes in declination in order to test how sure his students are of their knowledge. For it is a great proof of proficiency to understand the mistakes of others.

Now there are two parts to grammar. The first is called "me- 8 thodical" (that is, *methodos*), which lays out the paradigms of all the parts of speech; the other is called "historical," which gives a detailed treatment of historical knowledge and past achievements. One may learn these paradigms from many existing books, but the compendium of my excellent father will be of the greatest assistance in this regard; in it, there is nothing superfluous, and everything relevant to correct speaking is easily available.[17]

9   We would have the master adhere to the following practice: the boys should both write and practice orally the grammatical exercises they are set. If they only respond in writing, they will not know how to reply extemporaneously when called upon, as they will have grown used to thinking over every detail for a long time; but if, on the other hand, they are taught to respond from memory only, they will often not know the letters used to link the syllables.[18] But if, as we have said, they get used to doing both at the same time, they will attain an unencumbered facility in both writing and speaking, which will also be greatly increased by the habit of speaking continually in Latin.

10   I would like students, furthermore, to be taught certain general rules [of syntax], so that they may arrive more quickly as well as more surely at the rules' desired results. For example, students should master the difference between the verbs called "active" and "neutral" verbs, i.e., that there can be no passive forms of neutral verbs in either the first or second person when the speaker is an individual—that is, no one could say "I am ploughed, you are ploughed" and be correct.[19] Similarly I would have students observe the structure of the active verbs, of which there are said to be six classes; the first has only subject and object, while the others, in addition to the object in the accusative case, take the other cases in the order in which they stand, with the exception of the first [nominative] case.[20] Very little need be learned about the passives: just that, in every instance, subject and object exchange cases when verbs are converted [to the passive voice]. Teaching the neutral verbs is very easy, for they follow almost the same order and construction as the actives, except that their objects do not take the accusative, as do the actives; indeed the verbs called "transitive

neutrals" may take the accusative, but may not govern two words in the same case like active verbs.[21] Deponents follow the rule of the neutrals. I have given a few examples in order to make my meaning easier to understand.

It will be extremely useful, moreover, for the students to get used to writing elegantly while practicing these grammatical exercises, so that (for example) they usually end their sentences in a verb, and place dependent clauses before the clause they depend on, for [in this way] it will be easier to guide them into stylistic elegance afterwards. Since we assume a learned teacher, it is superfluous to specify that students should have accurate texts. In that compendium of my father's that I mentioned above, many people wanted to make numerous additions; they wanted fools to take them for experts, but the experts exposed them as fools.

But lest my motive should seem to be less love of truth than of detraction, let me give two relevant examples. You know the rule for comparatives: that nominative adjectives of the second declension are formed from the genitive plus [the ending] -or, with the exception of those having a vowel before a vowel.[22] This rule is commonly corrupted to read: "except those having a vowel before -us." Yet they say that *tenuis* and similar adjectives [of the third declension] whose stems end in vowels can be put into the comparative, as though the rule were not restricted to the second declension, where the only comparatives with stems ending in a vowel are those ending in -us; hence "stems ending in a vowel" and "stems before -us" both come down to the same thing. But they only reveal their own ignorance when they delete things they entirely fail to understand. This case is less bad, since no error is introduced, but their slipshod addenda about the use of patronymics and their spelling, like "Tytides," is perfectly intolerable. They have found the word written thus in corrupt manuscripts, I think, and so as to foster their own error and hide their ignorance under the authority of my father, they insert the form into his grammar. If they had had the merest taste of Greek they would have known that one must read Tydides, not "Tytides."

13   It is not enough, therefore, to run through these rules a single time; the students should return to them two or three times and more, if necessary, so that they know them like the backs of their hands, with instant recall. And it is perfectly sensible to call students back occasionally to repeat these rules even after they have passed on to more advanced studies, until they are so fixed in their minds that no interval of time, no occupation—however varied or important—can eradicate them.

14   Once they have mastered these rules, they must add a knowledge of quantity and prosody, a knowledge so useful that I daresay no one can rightly be called an educated man who does not possess it. That is why I cannot admire and praise enough the attentiveness and scrupulousness of the ancients, who were unwilling to leave behind small details such as these, even when thirsting after greatness. Even Augustine, the greatest pillar of our Church, wrote a book *On Music* where he explained the rules of metrics.[23] But, setting aside the authority of the ancients, the sheer usefulness, indeed the necessity, of this subject readily shows how zealously it should be acquired, for without this science no one is able to pronounce correctly—or, more importantly, to understand correctly. For we shall find many words in the poets that are in fact in different cases, though their endings sound alike, and anybody ignorant of prosody will not be able to tell between them, since some words will have an entirely different meaning which can only be recognized from the quantity of a single syllable.

15   In the end, even if it were totally useless, this knowledge should at least be desired for the sake of pleasure. Just as one takes greater pleasure in the lute-playing of someone who has achieved some knowledge of his art than in the playing of a tyro, so too, in reading the poets, one who understands versification is more touched

by their sweetness than someone who does not. Nor is this knowledge profitable in poetry alone, but also in what the rhetoricians call prose rhythm, which is based on metrical feet. Someone who cannot comprehend rhythmic prose will certainly be far less able to write it himself. For this purpose that book in verse which is attributed to Alexander[24] will not be without a certain utility, and students will also get from it a sense of the rules for past tenses, noun genders and declensions. Apart from the fact that he takes everything from Priscian, things written in verse are also more easily memorized and retained. In fact Priscian cannot in our view be correctly understood without knowing Greek (a subject we shall discuss shortly); but once students have acquired an initial experience with counting feet, commonly known as "scansion," they may master the rest of prosody from frequent reading of the poets. To this end they should commit Vergil's poetry to memory so as to learn the quantity of each syllable in accordance with the authority and example of the best of poets; they should also practice reciting them so that by constant repetition they may become aware of the quantity of the feet by merely chanting the words. The other kinds of verse they may learn from the authors who have written on this subject; they should leave nothing untouched in this most useful branch of knowledge.

Here I should like to issue a warning as from a watchtower — as 16 the satirist says,

trust me to recite a leaf of the sibyl to you.[25]

— indeed, I shall proclaim it loudly: no one can get completely to the bottom and into the marrow, so to speak, of prosody without knowledge of Greek. I know there are many people who say it is unnecessary for Latin literature. These are people who are themselves ignorant of Greek and want everyone else to be equally ignorant, so that if they may not be judged superior to others, at least they can avoid being thought inferior. For my part, I shall hold fast to this "error" (if error it be) as long as I live, and shall believe that Greek is not only useful but absolutely essential for Latin letters. Laying aside the fact that the Greekless often carelessly shorten letters that are long by nature because they grasp neither diphthongs nor the other norm of correct writing, i.e., orthography, we must recognize that a great part of our vocabulary takes its origin from that source, and that numerous passages may be found in our authors that someone ignorant of Greek will have no way of explaining. Vergil calls his descent to the underworld *Avernus*, a word taken from Greek, since birds are unable to fly above it safely[26] — something students will of course misunderstand unless they have learned that a bird [*avis*] is called *ornis* in Greek. Ovid says that the poison aconite arose from the saliva of Cerberus, "which country folk cautiously call aconite because it is born from hard, enduring rock."[27] Who will crack that nut without knowing that "rock" is called *akone* in Greek? Ovid says that Scylla, the daughter of Nisus, king of Megara, was turned into a bird and was called Ciris "from the cut hair,"[28] which no one, surely, will understand unless he has learned that "I cut" is *keiro* in Greek. In the *Fasti* the same author also asserts that Venus received her name from the foam of the sea;[29] this, too, students will not understand unless it is explained to them that "Aphrodite" is derived *apo tou aphrou*.

17   So they must confess that they are led even more by the awareness of their own ignorance than by the validity of their argument, if they recall that there are certain Greek inflexions in both the orators and the poets for which we have no rules in Latin. Vergil offers *luctificam Allecto*[30] and *nomine Dido / saepe vocaturum*,[31] and *Mantus filius*[32] in the accusative and genitive cases, and the orators offer *rhetoricen*, *dialecticen*, and other inflexions of this type. To enumerate the many instances of this kind is not germane to the present work. We follow the example of the learned men of old, none of whom was ignorant of Greek; and the authority of Quintilian,

who says that our literature flowed from the Greek;[33] and of Cicero, who holds that Greek literature should receive the credit if Cato speaks with more learning in [Cicero's] book *On Old Age* than he had been used to do in his own books;[34] and the exhortation of Horace, who urged:

page through the Greek models day and night

because

the Muse gave genius to the Greeks; to the Greeks she gave the ability to speak with smoothness and polish.[35]

I shall now indicate, as far as the judgement of my poor wit allows, how students may learn Greek. To be sure, it does not escape me that Quintilian instructs us to begin with the Greek authors. This seems too difficult to me for the following reason: Greek is not a natural language for us, so unless some beginning is first made in Latin, I do not know how children may be brought to learn Greek. So I persuade myself that Quintilian gave this advice because in his time everyone knew Latin, and there was no need to take great pains with it.[36] On the other hand, I have seen some students who, under the instruction of my best of fathers — a man whose great learning in Greek equalled his knowledge of Latin — after they had learned the basics in Latin, in one year had made so much progress in Greek that they were translating books into Latin at sight, all by themselves, and so correctly and faithfully that everyone was quick to applaud their efforts. Let students, then, acquire the Greek language, but not in the confused and disorderly way that the Greeks usually teach it. Instead, put into their hands the rules which Manuel Chrysoloras, our father's teacher, collected in summary form, or the ones which our father himself, a great lover of compendia, distilled from the rules of Chrysoloras.[37] And when teaching them they should be advised to derive the tenses of the verbs from a given general principle, and

18

let them know the verbs which the Greeks called *anomala*[38] [irregulars] like the the backs of their hands. For in this way it will be perfectly easy for them to distinguish, even at first glance, a noun from a verb and the tenses of the verb, which is very useful in that language; they will grasp this under frequent, careful questioning from their teacher.

19   Next they should gradually pass on to the authors. They should first take up the easier prose authors to ensure that they do not become bogged down with weighty thoughts and overlook what we chiefly want from them at first, [namely,] to strengthen their command of grammar. If some author proves particularly difficult, he should be given to them later on. Students should come next to Homer, the prince of poets, who is not difficult to learn, as he seems to have been a source for all our [Latin] writers. Their minds will delight in Vergil's imitation of him, for the *Aeneid* is like a mirror of Homer's works, and there is almost nothing in Vergil that does not have an analogue in Homer. And not only subject matter: they will also observe many verses translated word-for-word from that source. Vergil did the same thing, too, with Theocritus' *Idylls* and the *Works and Days* of Hesiod. Then let them work hard on the remaining writers of epic, tragedy, and comedy.

20   [In learning Greek] it is of primary importance for students to gather in the richness and variety of that language (whose vocabulary is surpassingly abundant), committing it not so much to memory as to writing. The words will lie readier to hand if they are set out in some order, and the sustained effort of writing will impress the words more on the mind, while the accents (of which that language is full) will be fully noted. Or if they should slip away (since memory is shaky), they will always have a place where they can be found, as in a treasury. For this reason it will of no small advantage if they have learned to write from the beginning and have had plenty of practice in it, and it will improve their

reading as well. Indeed, when they have made some progress, they must then begin to translate either from Greek into Latin or from Latin into Greek. This kind of exercise readily yields a vocabulary marked by propriety and distinction as well as facility and readiness of tongue. For many things which may be invisible to a reader are impossible for a translator to overlook.

Nevertheless, we do not want them completely to overlook 21 Latin while learning Greek. They might forget the former through lack of practice and might then have to start over again from the beginning. But once they have control of basic Greek grammar, let them continue on and study Priscian and the other [Latin] grammarians, where they will receive a more detailed treatment of matters they learned in brief form at the beginning. They will see that the authority of good authors permits many things that they had not known before owing to the short time they spent studying grammar. At the same time, they should compose declamations based on the letters of Cicero, which will give them a style that is both elegant and fluent, purity of diction and weight of learning; if they commit these letters to memory, they will later reap wonderful rewards with respect to ease of writing. Yet no one should think that the luxuriant style (which Cicero called "fat"[39]) depends on exercises in the *Letters* alone. A style like that comes from wide and varied reading. As Horace bears witness, "Knowledge is the source and principle of writing well."[40]

That is why it is now, at this juncture, that students should be 22 introduced to the other part of grammar which we have called "history." And just as they learned the other rules of grammar in summary form, so they should first peruse authors who have made selections of historical events. Typically Valerius Maximus and Justin will be placed in their hands, authors who will put before their mind's eye a nearly synoptic view of Roman and non-Roman history. Valerius Maximus will also offer the students the advantage of embellishing their style with examples pertaining to every part of virtue, to eminent words and deeds. Then they should read the remaining historians in order, from whom they will excerpt the customs, manners, and laws of various peoples, the various fortunes that befell individuals of genius and their vices and virtues. This practice is of great use in producing eloquence in daily speech and a reputation for prudence in a wide range of affairs.

23   About the same time they should survey all the poets in order, admiring the neatly contrived fictions that resemble reality, and they will relate these to the teachings about daily life that are hidden beneath their fabulous form. Cicero, indeed, maintains that poetical fictions were composed so that we might contemplate the likeness of everyday life under fictitious personages.[41] Even Saint Jerome, writing to Furia about preserving her widowhood,[42] held this view of Terence. While urging her to flee drunkenness, he cites the authority of the comic poet ("without Ceres and Bacchus, Venus grows cold"). "[Terence's] purpose," said Jerome, "was to know and describe human conduct."[43] From the poets students should [also] gather both the names and locations of rivers, mountains, cities, and countries.

24   Even Augustine's authority confirms that one should begin with Vergil. He writes as follows: "that is why children read Vergil, so that, having drunk in this great, most famous and best of all poets from their earliest years, they cannot lightly efface him through forgetfulness."[44] It makes sense, perhaps, to leave Lucan until after [the course in] rhetoric; as Quintilian says "he should be imitated by orators more than by poets."[45] Yet I freely confess that Lucan has this advantage: if you know him well, you can already be considered a learned man, especially as regards the deliberative genus.[46] His speeches are so grave and so artfully contrived that it is doubtful whether the precepts of rhetoric can be illustrated with greater clarity from anyone else. After Vergil, the *Thebaid* of Statius will follow immediately in order; since it was composed in imitation of the *Aeneid*, less effort will be required to learn it.

From the *Metamorphoses* of Ovid they may select the myths and little else, but to these myths they should apply themselves with great zeal, and they should understand that they are not appropriate only — as some think — for poets, for even Cicero regularly adorned both his speeches and his other books with myths as though they were jewels. They will take pleasure in Ovid's other works when they shall read them on their own; but they should at least have the *Fasti* at their disposal, in which certain lesser-known myths and histories and an account of the calendar are treated in considerable detail. Would that this book had come down to us in its entirety! For there is no other text which informs us more fully about the customs and religious rites of the ancients.

Seneca's tragedies are extremely helpful thanks to their myths 25 as well as their maxims. They are well suited to life and daily speech, for everything they contain is very serious, and they contain nothing frivolous or naughty. For purity and elegance of diction as well as propriety, no one is more suitable than Terence. Cicero will often use a saying of Terence, and Cicero's Laelius expressly affirms his pleasure in using him.[47] Hence he must be committed to memory through sustained reading. Nor am I afraid to pair him with Juvenal, the prince of satirists. With these two authors at one's disposal, one may be confident, not only of being able to hold forth elegantly on any subject that arises in day-to-day speech, but also of having some maxim suitable for every subject. And no one should be deterred from reading that satirist because in some places he attacks certain horrible vices too explicitly. First of all, he only does this occasionally, and second, we ought to abhor vicious people more than those who attack the vices. Once those blemishes have been removed (and they are few, as we have said), we shall find nothing which is not praiseworthy and perfectly suitable for a Christian. Plautus will be of great profit, not only for his witticisms, which embellish life, but also for his eloquence. The ancients rated him so highly that they used to claim that "if the Muses had wanted to speak Latin, they would have spoken like Plautus."[48] Macrobius also asserts that the two most eloquent men of ancient times were "the comic playwright Plautus and the orator Cicero."[49] Horace in my opinion, in addition to his excellent understanding of the art of poetry, will also reinforce propriety of diction, nor will you easily find anyone who sticks closer to Vergil in the fashioning of epithets. In addition Persius provides us with much that is relevant to understanding the other satirists. Though he is, to be sure, elliptical and obscure, he nevertheless compensates for this with the variety of his subject matter.

26   The other poets are not, indeed, without their uses, but are more appropriately studied at another time. However, since much in the poets has been taken from astrology and geography, it will be desirable for students to know thoroughly the treatise *On the Sphere*,[50] and to look at Pomponius Mela, Hyginus, Solinus, Martianus Capella, and Strabo (whom my father recently translated into Latin).[51] For this purpose it will also be extremely useful to familiarize students with Ptolemy's world-map, so that in describing various locations they may place that image before their mind's eyes and seem to be gazing on the real thing, as though they were actually present. Describing the world in any other way is usually a source of confusion.

27   By now, I think, it is perfectly clear that anyone trained in the aforesaid studies is ready to pass on to the discipline of rhetoric. Once he has acquired the art of speaking, not only will he understand the speeches of Cicero, but, as a result of the variety of things he has learned already, he will now also possess a rich vocabulary and a highly wrought, artistic style. No text is more useful or convenient for learning this discipline than the *Rhetorica ad Herennium* of Cicero, where all the parts of rhetoric are set forth, perfectly and succinctly.[52] Declamations should even be composed upon certain readings in it; all instruction ought to adapt itself to practical exercises. Afterwards it will be a simple thing to master

Cicero's other books on the education of the orator, and to observe those precepts in the mirror of his speeches. Similarly, it will be easy, too, to survey the works of Quintilian, who is extremely good on this subject.

All the books of Cicero are to be read regularly, and they are all 28 so useful and easy that they should never be laid aside. They are full of moral philosophy (which for orators, too, is a vital subject). It will be best if students also master logic and Aristotle's *Ethics*, then the dialogues of Plato. Cicero himself seems to have imbibed everything from Plato's springs and to have imitated him so thoroughly that the Roman writer even names some of his dialogues after their principal interlocutors and their subject matter, as Plato did. All Cicero's books are of surpassing excellence and usefulness, but in my view primacy should be granted to the book *On Duties* and to the *Tusculans*, the former for its precepts suited to every aspect of life, the latter for the wide range of knowledge it contains as well as for its precepts, which liberally supply us with an abundance [of topics] on almost every subject one may write about. If students are going to be introduced to civil law, rhetoric will prove highly useful in the analysis of judicial cases and in the explanation of many passages. Once they have acquired all this, they no longer need a teacher, but are themselves ready to teach others. They will be able to read and understand on their own.

For the rest, since we have shown with sufficient fullness, I 29 think, how teachers should instruct their students, it remains to explain how youths should conduct themselves in their studies. We lay it down that the first and healthiest of precepts, at which everything may be aimed as though at a target (or *skopos*, as the Greeks would say) is this: young people should bear in mind that at some point they themselves will be teachers.[53] Someone who thinks that he need never render account of his studies will skip many things and will run through most things lightly and, as they say, superficially, with unwashed feet;[54] he will not try to look into anything deeply, down to its essence. But someone who believes that he will have to teach what he has learned will leave nothing untouched or undiscussed; he will imagine all possible questions coming up as though conducting a dialogue with himself and will try to elicit the truth in disputation. Also, if students have someone to whom, for the sake of practice, they may relate what they have heard, nothing will be more useful; for as Quintilian says, the best way to make progress is to teach what you have learned.

30 Let them not be satisfied with listening to the teacher only, but let them study for themselves the commentators on the authors and mark "down to the roots," as they say, their maxims and the force of words. Let them look for new maxims with specific applications. Writing glosses in books is also extremely profitable, the more so if they have some hope of publishing them someday, for we are more careful with such things when we are in pursuit of praise. Writing of this kind wonderfully sharpens the wit, polishes the tongue, produces fluency in writing, leads to precise factual knowledge, strengthens the memory, and, finally, affords students a storeroom, as it were, of commentary and memory aids.

31 Once they begin to study on their own, they should make an effort to read miscellaneous works like Gellius, Macrobius' *Saturnalia*, and Pliny's *Natural History* (a book no less varied than Nature herself). To this list we may add Augustine's *City of God*, a work filled with historical information as well as material on the rites and religion of the ancients.[55] But they should hold fast to the practice of always making excerpts of what they read, and they should convince themselves of the truth of Pliny's dictum, that "there is no book so bad that it is totally useless."[56] The ancients had such regard for this plan of study that Pliny the Elder left to his nephew 160 notebooks of selected passages, written on both sides of the page, which on one occasion in Spain the elder Pliny could have sold to Larcius Licinus for 400,000 sesterces.[57] Let them excerpt those things in particular which seem worth remem-

bering and are rarely found. This practice will also serve greatly to develop a rich and ready diction if students, in the course of their miscellaneous reading, will note down maxims pertinent to a given topic and collect them in one particular place, reviewing at night any excellent thing they have read or heard during the day, like the Pythagoreans. The process stamps these ideas into memory so strongly that they can be expunged only with the greatest difficulty, and the stamping will be stronger still if they refresh their recollection of all the precepts on some fixed day of the month.

In Greek they will make rapid progress so long as they do not always expect a teacher to be their guide (after they have acquired the basics). They should study on their own, using, in place of a teacher, books that have been translated into Latin. They can pick up the vocabulary themselves from following the Latin and comparing it with the Greek. There are some texts, especially sacred books, where a verse in the Latin translation is not a syllable longer or shorter than the Greek original. Such texts are admirably adapted for this purpose, and I have known certain men who, without having any teacher at all, have achieved a profound knowledge of Greek using this method.

They will have to read Greek assiduously, for if Latin slips away from us through disuse, what must we infer about a language which is not natural to us? Students should not read to themselves or mumble under their breath, for it often happens that someone who can't hear even himself will skip over numerous verses as though he were somewhere else. Reading out loud is of no small benefit to the understanding, since of course what sounds like a voice from outside makes our ears spur the mind sharply to attention. It even helps our digestion somewhat, or so authorities on the secrets of nature and medicine claim. As even Plutarch reports, the voice, which is a movement of air, strengthens the intestines (not on the surface but from within), increases heat and thins the blood, cleans out all the veins and opens the arteries, and

32

33

allows no unnecessary moisture to stand motionless in those vessels which take in and digest food.[58] Pliny also says that he reads Greek and Latin over and over, out loud and with concentration, not for the sake of his voice but of his stomach;[59] Ariston also used to say "neither a bath nor a speech is of any use unless it removes impurities."[60] Nevertheless one must take care lest the voice become booming and forced; too much strain will disrupt it and even leads to hoarseness. In general if students get used to reading in a large group, this will produce boldness in giving speeches, something many lack in our day, as we see; then again Isocrates, whom Cicero did not hesitate to call the "father of eloquence,"[61] is said to have been so inexperienced in this area that he could not deliver a single speech from memory.

34   While reading one should not stop before reaching the end of the sentence, which is called a *clausula*;[62] if at the first encounter, as they say, the sentence is not understood, one should retreat and reread it two and three times more attentively, until the sense is obediently driven out by the diligence of the assailant. Students should *not* do what we have heard a certain person did years ago when reading Cicero's *On the Orator*—that is, admire only the words and the order of expression while completely missing the sense. One should rather imitate very thirsty men who do not stop to admire the embossed work and the embellishments on cups when quenching a burning thirst. So students should first take in ideas and moral content, then turn to flowers of language. There are certain animals that feed on the flower, like bees; certain ones on the branches, like goats; and certain ones on the roots, like pigs. Let the student take as his models those who consume all these things. Let him note what is said with distinction and originality in the narrative; he should attend to the purity and elegance of the composition; and he should mark down maxims that encapsulate courage, prudence, justice, and modesty.

He should think of poetry as having effects similar to those re-   35
ported of an octopus' head. For authorities on natural secrets say
octopus head is delicious when added to a dish, but it affects the
mind with oppressive visions and the most violent apparitions.
Likewise poetry nourishes the human mind with food of the
greatest sweetness, but one ingests with it an equal portion of disorder and agitation. Consequently one must rein in the mind
while reading and not be so swept along by enthusiasm for myths
that these fantasies are understood nakedly, as it were.[63] They
should be probed individually for whatever utility they may yield
under analysis. Students should respect the attitude of Cato—
which is also that of Xenophon writing about Cyrus—who as a
boy would always obey the commands of his teacher, but would
always ask that the reason for the command be explained to him.[64]
Impious, cruel, unjust or shameful statements in the poets are not
to be set down to vice, but considered from the artistic point of
view as observing the decorum proper to each character. We see
this happen in other matters as well: there are things the mind
shrinks from when they appear to be real, but we think about
them or hear about them with pleasure when we know they are
strictly fictional. Our Chrysoloras, we understand, used to say
that we take great pleasure in seeing scorpions and snakes accurately painted, though we run from the real thing; we are annoyed
when we hear the grunting of a pig, the whirring of a saw, the
whistling of the wind, the roar of the sea, but we take a certain
pleasure in hearing someone imitate these noises with his voice.
But we should commit to memory whatever we find in the authors
that is adaptable to our way of life and whatever pertains to the rational exercise of the virtues.

Above all one must apply order to the process of study. Stu-   36
dents should not engage in indiscriminate reading of miscellaneous books. They should establish fixed hours for particular

readings. This is the single most useful practice for achieving a range of reading and for finishing tasks. Its value will be easily and abundantly understood if someone will read or write a little bit at a fixed hour and do it without fail; after a few days he will see how much he has accomplished. Hesiod intones this very thing (as translated by my father):

If you try to add small things to tiny things,
and do this often, a great heap accumulates.[65]

But it may be learned from other cases that nothing is more useless, nothing uglier than disorder, especially the kind the Greeks call *ataxia*. A chorus is made up of many different people who would produce an inharmonious noise, confused and unpleasant to the ears, if they each decided to sing as the spirit led them. But when each one sings at the correct time and place as instructed, a pleasing and unanimous harmony bursts forth from their multiplied sound. In an army one may see the same thing. If soldiers wander about at random without paying attention to their formations, they give the enemy an easy victory and the eye a shameful spectacle; when knights, footsoldiers, carts, servants, and baggage move about promiscuously, they become an obstacle even to themselves if a battle breaks out. On the other hand a well ordered army instills hope in its friends and fear in its enemies when they see knights, squires, archers, and slingers proceeding each in his own place and preserving order. Hence let us conclude that this kind of order is of no less use in regulating our literary study than it is in other matters. For unless our time is apportioned for [particular] readings, the mind will be distracted by the multitude of books. As a result of trying to take in many things at the same time and embrace them simultaneously in thought, we give independent and concentrated thought to no part of our reading. Furthermore, since what we learn during the day should be recalled in the evening, we shall probably fail to gather what we have read in each book under a single purview, without any hesitation or error, unless everything comes to us in distinct portions.

We shall add one last thing—last in our system but not last in 37 the benefit it confers—which, nevertheless, we wish to be understood less as a precept than as a counsel. That is, that students should consider nothing sweeter than this literary leisure which, as Cicero says, "motivates an adolescent and delights old age; it adds embellishment to good fortune and offers refuge and solace in adversity; it delights at home and does not distract from public affairs."[66] For this reason students should allow no time to slip from them empty of study; let this be their business, their work, and their rest; let them devote their waking hours, even their sleep, to their studies. For what more honorable thing can they do, when they want leisure, than to spend their leisure in study, an activity everyone has always considered both highly useful and exceedingly pleasant? Let students devote the same amount of time to reviewing their studies that others devote to gambling, sport, or spectacles. There they will not lack sights and spectacles, marvels and men to admire; so long as they are there they will regret nothing they have heard and nothing they have said. No one there will snipe at anyone maliciously, and they themselves will criticize no one. They will not be worried by empty hopes or fears, nor upset by rumors. They shall speak only with themselves and with men of peace; they shall even speak with the dead, a thing denied to the others. This is the life that Pliny the Younger called princely and pure; this is the leisure he praised as "sweet and honorable and more attractive than almost any employment";[67] this is what Atilius referred to when, combining wit and wisdom, he said that "it was preferable to have no work to do than to work at nothing."[68]

This was why Pliny the Elder thought that all time not ex- 38 pended in study was lost. He was so careful of his time that he is said to have often censured the younger Pliny, his sister's son, because he was taking a walk, on the grounds that it was a waste of time.[69] Once, indeed, when he was having something read aloud in the manner of the ancients and the reader, whom the Greeks call *anagnostes*, "had pronounced some things incorrectly, one of his friends stopped him and had the passage read again." Pliny said to him, "Had you not understood? And when he had admitted that he had," [Pliny continued] "why, then, did you stop him? We have lost ten more verses because of your interruption."[70] Cato, too, who after his death was called Uticensis is said to have been in the habit of reading in the vestibule of the senate house so as not to lose time in the interval while the senate was being convened.[71] Theophrastus is said to have rebuked Nature because she had given long life to crows and deer who had no need to live a long time, but a short life to men, who need many ages to learn an infinite number of things.[72] It is his business whether it is fitting for a serious philosopher to make such a complaint, but let us for our part hold to this opinion, that the time Theophrastus lamented was too brief must not be spent in vain. Other animate creatures have powers innate to them, like the power of running in horses and flying in birds, but to mankind has been given the desire to know, which is also where the humanities get their name. For what the Greeks call *paideia* we call learning and instruction in the liberal arts. The ancients also called this *humanitas*, since devotion to knowledge has been given to the human being alone out of all living creatures. This kind of study is more varied than the other branches of knowledge. But I hope that those who are now [at the stage of] understanding literature on their own will have acquired such pleasure from their studies that they will have little need of our urgings. Let this, then, be the limit of our essay.

39   You have, my dear Maffeo, a gift from your teacher which will be seen to have much more utility hidden within it than it seems to promise on the surface. For this is the program of teaching and the precepts of study which my father, who was as learned as he

was excellent — your grandfather, as it were, in literary study[73] — used to teach his pupils. You will consider them the best precepts for this one reason in particular: that absolute princes of letters have sprung forth from his school as though from the Trojan horse. Indeed, the majority of those who have cultivated literary study both in our Italy and in the rest of the world have flowed out from his springs. If, then, with your whole heart (as they say) you apply yourself to following these precepts, you will yield so much fruit from thence that you will be able not only to sustain and preserve, but even to surpass the hope for you that your natural ability promises and that the estimation of your talent has aroused.

At Verona, 15 February 1459

NOTE ON THE TRANSLATIONS

NOTES

BIBLIOGRAPHY

INDEX

Note on the Translations

෨ඁ෨

The translation of Vergerio's *The Character and Studies Befitting a Free-Born Youth* is based on that of Attilio Gnesotto, "Petri Pauli Vergerii *De ingenuis moribus et liberalibus studiis adulescentiae*," *Atti e memorie della R. Accademia di Scienze Lettere ed Arti in Padova*, n.s. 34 (1917), 75–156 at 95–146. Carlo Miani, "Petri Pauli Vergerii—ad Ubertinum de Carraria *De ingenuis moribus et liberalibus adolescentiae studiis liber*," *Atti e memorie della Società istriana di archeologia e storia patria* 72–73, n.s. 20–21 (1972–73), 183–251, has also been consulted. The translation of Bruni's *The Study of Literature* is based on the Latin text in Paolo Viti (ed.), *Opere letterarie e politiche di Leonardo Bruni* (Turin: Unione Tipografico-Editrice Torinese, 1996), 248–79. The translation of Piccolomini's treatise is based on that of Rudolf Wolkan, *Die Briefwechsel des Eneas Silvius Piccolomini*, Fontes rerum Austriacarum, Diplomataria et acta, 61–62, 67–68, 4 vols. (Vienna: A. Holder, 1909–1918), 67 [II Abteilung, 1912]: 103–158 [= text 40]. Wolkan's text was reprinted in E. Garin, *Il pensiero pedagogico dello Umanesimo* (Florence: Giuntine and Sansoni, 1958), 198–295, with a few minor corrections; Garin's text has been consulted in preparing the present text. For the translation of Battista Guarino's *A Program of Teaching and Learning*, the edition in Garin's *Il pensiero pedagogico*, 434–70 has been used.

English versions of these four treatises may be found in William Harrison Woodward, *Vittorino da Feltre and Other Humanist Educators* (Cambridge: Cambridge University Press, 1897; rpt. New York: Columbia University, 1963; Toronto: University of Toronto Press, 1996). Woodward's versions, however, are notoriously loose and some sections of the original text are not translated at all, so that his renderings are more paraphrases than translations. Thus the translations of the treatises by Vergerio and Battista Guarino in this volume may be counted as the first complete, close renderings into English. The translation of the Bruni treatise printed here is that of James Hankins, taken from *The Humanism of Leonardo Bruni: Selected Texts*, Gordon Griffiths, James Hankins, and David Thompson (eds.), Medieval and Renaissance Texts and Studies, 46

(Binghamton, NY: MRTS, 1987), 240–51, which has been checked and slightly modified. Nelson's translation of the Piccolomini treatise has been used as a starting point, but has been thoroughly revised.

The annotations of Gnesotto, Hankins, Wolkan, Nelson, and Garin have provided indispensable starting points for the notes to the translations. In each case, however, the original set of notes has been carefully reworked: references have been checked, some notes have been eliminated, further citations have been identified, and a few explanatory notes added.

Notes

ABBREVIATIONS

PL   J.-P. Migne, *Patrologiae cursus completus . . . series latina*, 221 vols. (Paris: J.-P. Migne, 1844–64).

Keil   Heinrich Keil (ed.), *Grammatici latini*, 7 vols. (Leipzig: Teubner, 1857–80).

THE CHARACTER AND STUDIES BEFITTING A FREE-BORN YOUTH

1. Ubertino da Cararra (1390–1407), third son of Francesco Novello and Taddea d'Este, was a member of the ruling family of Padua and took an active part in the military adventures of his day until his untimely death. His grandfather, Francesco da Carrara (the elder), was Signore of Padua from 1355 to 1388.

2. Cicero *Sen.* 3.8; Plato *Resp.* 329E-330A; Plutarch *Them.* 18.3.

3. Seneca *De ira* 2.18.2; ps. Plutarch *De educ.* 5; Aristotle *Eth. Nic.* 2.1.8.

4. Ps. Plutarch *De educ.* 11.

5. Seneca *Clem.* 1.8.1.

6. Francesco Novello was preceded as Signore of Padua by Francesco (the elder), Jacopino, Jacopo II, Marsilietto, and Ubertino.

7. Sallust *Cat.* 1.4; Seneca *Constant.* 5.4–5.

8. Cicero *Q Fr.* 1.1.36.

9. Quintilian *Inst.* 2.8.1.

10. Quintilian *Inst.* 1.3.7; Cicero *Sen.* 23.82; idem *Arch.* 11.26.

11. Xenophon *Mem.* 4.1.3, although Vergerio may have taken this reference from an intermediary source.

12. I.e., they cannot grasp the Platonic idea of virtue using their reason.

13. Cicero *Off.* 1.5.15; Plato *Phdr.* 250D.

14. Quintilian *Inst.* 2.9.1–2.

15. Aristotle *De an.* 2.9.

16. Plutarch *Con. prae.* 25; Diogenes Laertius 2.33.

17. Sallust *Iug.* 4.

18. Suetonius *Iul.* 7.

19. Seneca *Ep.* 6.5–6, 11.8–10.

20. Quintilian *Inst.* 1.2.5; Cicero *Off.* 1.34.122.

21. Ps. Plutarch *De educ.* 4, 12.

22. Aristotle *Rh.* 2.12.6.

23. Ibid. 2.12.8, 2.13.7.

24. See Aristotle *Eth. Nic.* 4.1–2.

25. Aristotle *Eth. Nic.* 4.3.3–7.

26. Aristotle *Rh.* 2.12.8–9.

27. Horace *Ars P.* 163.

28. Aristotle *Rh.* 2.12.6–7.

29. Ibid. 2.12.14.

30. Ps. Plutarch *De educ.* 14.

31. Ibid.

32. Jerome *Ep.* 70 (*PL* XXII 665); idem *Comm. in Epist. ad Galat.* (*PL* XXVI 389); idem *Comm. in Epist. ad Eph.* (*PL* XXVI 525); or idem *Comm. in Epist. ad Titum* (*PL* XXVI 571), which indicate that St. Paul's source was Menander.

33. Aristotle *Rh.* 2.12.10.

34. Ibid. 2.12.7.

35. Ibid. 2.12.4.

36. Terence *An.* 1.1.60–61.

37. Aristotle *Rh.* 2.12.7, 15.

38. Ibid. 2.12.13.

39. Aristotle *Pol.* 8.1.1–2; idem *Eth. Nic.* 10.9.8.

40. Aristotle *Rh.* 2.12.3; Cicero *Sen.* 11.36; idem *Off.* 1.34.122.

41. Aristotle *Rh.* 2.13.6, 13.

42. Cicero *Sen.* 12.39–41.

43. Seneca *Ep.* 10.2, 25.5.

44. Seneca *Clem.* 2.7.4; ps. Plutarch *De educ.* 7.

45. Seneca *Helv.* 10.11.

46. Seneca *Ep.* 83.17–18; idem *De ira,* 2.20.2.

47. Plutarch *Lyc.* 28.8; idem *Dem.* 1.4.

48. Cicero *Off.* 1.30.106.

49. Seneca *Oct.* 454.

50. Matt. 5:33–35 (Vulg.).

51. Valerius Maximus 2.1.9.

52. Cicero *Amic.* 24.88–25.95.

53. Cicero *Off.* 1.26.91.

54. Matt. 19:21–24 (Vulg.); Jerome *Comm.* (PL XXVI 142–43).

55. Plato *Grg.* 526 A (a work translated by Vergerio).

56. Quintilian *Inst.* 1.2.6.

57. Seneca *Ep.* 88.2.

58. Quintilian *Inst.* 1.1.15–19.

59. No source has been located for this anecdote. Suspicion centers on Vergerio's admission that "the name of each, however, is unknown": Gnesotto, *ad loc.* speculates that either Vergerio himself had been the young man here, or that he made up the story.

60. Ps. Plutarch *De educ.* 4.

61. Vergil *Georg.* 3.165.

62. Quintilian *Inst.* 1.1.19.

63. Seneca *Ep.* 76.3.

64. Valerius Maximus 8.7.1; Cicero *Sen.* 8.26.

65. Quintilian *Inst.* 1.10.13; Valerius Maximus 8.7.ext.8; Cicero *Sen.* 8.26.

66. Vergerio is more severe than ps. Plutarch *De educ.* 12 and Seneca *Clem.* 1.16.3.

67. Seneca *De ira* 2.21.3; Quintilian *Inst.* 2.4.10.

68. Aristotle [*Pr.*] 30.1; Cicero *Tusc.* 1.33.80.

69. Cicero *Off.* 1.32.118.

70. Vergil *Aen.* 6.129–30.

71. Cicero *Off.* 1.32.118.

72. Ps. Aurelius Victor *Ep. de Caes.*, 41.8.

73. Plato *Resp.* 473C-D; Cicero *Q Fr.* 1.10.29; Valerius Maximus 7.2.ext.4; Lactantius *Div. Inst.* 3.21.

74. Suetonius *Claud.* 41–42; idem *Ner.* 52.

75. Seneca *Clem.* 2.1.2; Suetonius *Ner.* 10.

76. According to Suetonius, Nero's pretended clemency took the form of wishing that he were ignorant of letters so as to be unable to sign orders for execution.

77. Cicero *Sen.* 3.9; idem *Arch.* 7.16.

78. Ps. Plutarch *De educ.* 10.

79. Suetonius *Dom.* 3.1; Aurelius Victor *Caes.* 11.5; ps. Aurelius Victor *Ep. de Caes.* 11.6.

80. Aurelius Victor *Caes.* 10.6, 11.2.; ps. Aurelius Victor *Ep. de Caes.* 10.16.

81. Seneca *Clem.* 1.8.1.

82. Suetonius *Dom.* 3; Aurelius Victor *Caes.* 11.6.

83. I.e., when the 'hunting season' for flies was over.

84. Cicero *Off.* 3.1.1.

85. Cicero *Fin.* 3.2.7; Plutarch *Cat. Min.* 19.1; Valerius Maximus 8.7.2.

86. Quintilian *Inst.* 2.18.4.

87. Cicero *Fam.* 9.1.

88. Cicero *Arch.* 3.5.

89. Vergerio was undoubtedly thinking of the students of Manuel Chrysoloras, a Greek émigré who taught a number of Italian scholars (including Leonardo Bruni, Uberto Decembrio, and Vergerio himself) during his various sojourns in Italy.

90. Seneca *Ep.* 88.2.

91. Quintilian *Inst.* 2.15.33.

92. Aristotle *Pol.* 8.2.3.

93. Ibid. 8.2.6, 8.3.2.

94. Ibid. 8.3.1; Cicero *Arch.* 7.16.

95. Quintilian *Inst.* 1.4.5.

96. Ibid. 2.17.2.

97. Aristotle's division of rhetoric into three genres (*Rh.* 1.3.3) is carried over into later writers like Quintilian *Inst.* 2.21.23.

98. Quintilian *Inst.* 2.21.5.

99. Aristotle *Rh.* 1.11.23.

100. See note 65 above.

101. Quintilian *Inst.* 1.10.

102. Ibid. 1.12.18.

103. I.e., theology.

104. Vergerio is referring here to metaphysics, as he explains two paragraphs later.

105. Seneca *Ep.* 88.36.

106. Cicero *Arch.* 1.2.

107. Quintilian *Inst.* 11.2.1.

108. Ibid. 11.2.1; Dante *Paradiso* 5.41–42.

109. Prudential knowledge, in the Aristotelian system, is equivalent to moral philosophy.

110. Quintilian *Inst.* 2.8.7.

111. Aristotle *Pol.* 8.2.2; see also Seneca *Ep.* 88.37.

112. Ps. Plutarch *De educ.* 10.

113. Quintilian *Inst.* 1.1.23.

114. Vergil *Georg.* 2.272.

115. Quintilian *Inst.* 2.3.

116. Seneca *Ep.* 2, 45.1, 108; here Vergerio stands in opposition to Quintilian *Inst.* 1.12.1–7.

117. Quintilian *Inst.* 1.3.1–7.

118. Cicero *Sen.* 11.38.

119. Cicero *Sen.* 13.43–45; Quintilian *Inst.* 1.2.17–29.

120. This reference to Quintilian has not been located.

121. (Perhaps) Plutarch *De Alex. fort.* 1.4.

122. Suetonius *Iul.* 56; idem *Aug.* 84.1.

123. Seneca *Ep.* 117.32; idem *De brev. vit.* 3.2.

124. Cicero *Off.* 1.7.23–24, 1.12.38.

125. Homer *Il.* 3.179; Xenophon *Mem.* 3.2.2; Plutarch *De Alex. fort.* 1.10; idem *Alex.* 8.2.

126. Cicero *Tusc.* 2.14.34.

127. Francesco Novello was Signore of Padua from 1390 until 1405.

128. Cicero *Sen.* 19.69–70.

129. Seneca *Ep.* 93.2–3, 70.4, 77; idem *Ben.* 3.31.4; idem *De brev. vit.* passim.

130. Valerius Maximus 5.4.2.

131. Ibid. 3.1.1.

132. Ubertino was eleven years old.

133. Ubertino's role at the battle of Brescia (24 October 1401), in which Gian Galeazzo defeated the imperial army, is only attested in contemporary sources written by Vergerio.

134. I.e., where sanctuary could normally be expected.

135. Seneca *Prov.* 4.11; Plutarch *Lyc.* passim; Cicero *Tusc.* 2.14.34, 5.27.77.

136. Plutarch, *Apoph. Lac.* 16, 17 (241F).

137. Cicero *Tusc.* 2.16.37.

138. Perhaps ps. Aurelius Victor *Ep. de Caes.* 48.

139. Aristotle *Pol.* 8.4.1.

140. Ibid. 8.4.2.

141. Plutarch *Mar.* 34.3.

142. Valerius Maximus 2.3.2.

143. Horace *Carm.* 3.2.1–6.

144. E.g., Vegetius *Mil.*; Frontinus *Str.*

145. Suetonius *Aug.* 64.

146. Valerius Maximus, 8.8.1–2.

147. Horace *Sat.* 2.2.12.

148. Plutarch *Lyc.* 24.4–25.3, 12.6–11.

149. Quintilian *Inst.* 9.4.12.

150. Valerius Maximus 8.8.ext.2; Plutarch *De Alex. fort.* 1.10; Homer *Il.* 9.186–89.

151. Vergerio is describing the musical practices of his own day, but with an eye on Aristotle *Pol.* 8.5.8.

152. Ibid. 8.6.5, 7–8; Plutarch *Alc.* 2.5–6.

153. (Perhaps) Philostratus *Her.* 11.2.

154. Suetonius *Claud.* 33.

155. Cicero *Off.* 3.1.1.

156. Ibid. 1.36.130.

157. Perhaps a turn on Cicero's words to his brother Quintus (*Q Fr.* 1.1.36), *At ea quidem, quae supra scripta sunt, non ut te instituerem, scripsi.*

THE STUDY OF LITERATURE

1. The dedicatee, Battista di Montefeltro (1384–1448), was a famous woman scholar of the Renaissance and the wife of Galeazzo Malatesta, the lord of Pesaro.

2. Cicero *Brut.* 211; Quintilian *Inst.* 1.1.6.

3. Demetrius *Eloc. passim*, esp. 127; Ovid *Ep. Sapph.*

4. Plato *Menex.* 235E-136D.

5. "Liberal," also "native"; the implication may be that such learning is native to Italy, unlike the scholastic theology of the north.

6. The necessity for both these elements in the orator's education was emphasized by Cicero *De or.* 1.6.20, and *passim*.

7. Cf. Quintilian's doctrine of imitation in *Inst.* 10.2.

8. Possibly a hit at Ambrogio Traversari (1386–1429), a learned Camaldulensian monk and a rival of Bruni's, of whose translations from the Greek Fathers Bruni disapproved.

9. *Periodos, kolon,* and *komma* are technical terms in Greek rhetoric which refer, respectively, to a complete sense unit (or *sententia* in Latin), to a clause within that sentence, and to a short phrase within the clause. See Cicero *Orat.* 62.211; Quintilian *Inst.* 9.4.27.

10. Vergil *Aen.* 5.556. The point is that without a knowledge of quantity (and meter, as he might have added), it is hard to distinguish the ablative and nominative cases, which in the present instance are spelled alike. One might otherwise read, "As usual, they all got haircuts from the tight-fitting crowns."

11. Cicero *De or.* 3.43.173–76.

12. Aristotle *Rh.* 3.8; Cicero *De or.* 3.47.182–83; idem *Orat.* 57.191–92. The *clausula* was a rhythmic conclusion to a clause or period.

13. Cicero *Orat.* 58.197, 63.213, 64.218.

14. Technical terms in rhetoric; see ibid. 36.126; Quintilian *Inst.* 3.6, 4.4.1.

15. Cicero *Orat.* 17.56; idem *De orat.* 3.56.213; idem *Brut.* 142.

16. See Bruni's *Isagogue of Moral Philosophy*, in *The Humanism of Leonardo Bruni*, Griffiths, Hankins, and Thompson, eds., 267–82, for further discussion of these points.

17. Cicero *De or.* 3.22.82–23.89.

18. Homer *Il.* 6.77 ff. Bruni has confused Hector with Helenus.

19. Ibid. 2.23–35. Bruni has again confused the story: Zeus sends to Agamemnon a dream, not the goddess Iris. This may be a owing to a corruption in his Greek manuscript of the word *oneiros* to *Iris*.

20. Vergil *Aen.* 6.724–31.

21. Vergil *Ecl.* 4.4–7.

22. A combination of a poet and a seer.

23. Lactantius *Div. inst.* 7.24.11–12.

24. The Pythagoreans. Bruni would have been familiar with their theory from Plato *Meno* 85e ff., and Diogenes Laertius 8.1–50.

25. Carlo Malatesta (1364–1429), ruler of Rimini, a famous condottiere. There is an old story that he allowed an ancient statue of Vergil by the river Mincio to be destroyed after the battle of Governolo, on 28 August 1397, as a result of which he was roundly condemned for being an opponent of humanistic studies; see Alan Fisher, "Three Meditations on the Destruction of Vergil's Statue: The Early Humanist Theory of Poetry," *Renaissance Quarterly*, 40 (1987), 607–35.

26. Homer *Od.* 2.50, 2.85–128, 19, 23.

27. Euripides *Alc.* passim, esp. 152–98, 282–86.

28. Ovid *Met.* 1.452–567.

29. Homer *Od.* 8.266–366; Vergil *Aen.* 8.369–406.

30. Jud. 16.19 (Vulg.).

31. Gen. 19.31–38 (Vulg.).

32. Ibid. 13:13, 18:20–19:29.

33. 2 Sam. 11:3–4 (Vulg.).

34. 1 Reg. 2:24–25 (Vulg.).

35. 1 Reg. 11:1 (Vulg.)

36. Vergil *Aen.* 4.

37. Cicero *De or.* 1.5.17.

THE EDUCATION OF BOYS

1. John of Salisbury *Policraticus* 5.7 (*PL CIC* 554B-C).

2. Eccles. 10.31 (Vulg.)

3. Prov. 8.15 (Vulg.).

4. Juvenal 8.30–32.

5. Ibid. 8.56–57.

6. Ibid. 8.76–77.

7. John of Salisbury *Policraticus* 4.6 (*PL CIC* 524D, 525C–D).

8. Boethius *De philos. consol.* 1.4; John of Salisbury *Policraticus* 4.6 (*PL CIC* 525D); Plato *Resp.* 473D.

9. Ps. Plutarch *De educ.* 10.

10. Gen. 27.27 (Vulg.)

11. Kaspar Wendel, Ladislas' teacher, was a priest of the town of Gars (Bavaria) in 1450.

12. Act. 3.6 (Vulg.)

13. A paraphrase of Prov. 8.19 (Vulg.).

14. Quintilian *Inst.* 1.1.1–3.

15. Ps. Plutarch *De educ.* 4.

16. The argument is that since body is created before soul, the care of the body should naturally be treated before the care of the mind.

17. Cicero *Fam.* 1.6.2.

18. Quintilian *Inst.* 1.9.5, where the anecdote is told about Crates.

19. Ibid. 1.1.9.

20. Ibid. 1.1.8.

21. Ibid. 1.1.23.

22. Ps. Plutarch *De educ.* 7.

23. Quintilian *Inst.* 2.2.5.

24. Ibid. 2.3.2–3.

25. Ps. Plutarch *De educ.* 7.

26. Quintilian *Inst.* 1.3.13.

27. Juvenal 7.210–11.

28. Ps. Plutarch *De educ.* 12; Quintilian *Inst.* 1.3.14–17.

29. Quintilian *Inst.* 2.2.8, 2.9.1–2.

30. Juvenal 7.207–10.

31. Ps. Plutarch *De educ.* 11.

32. Quintilian *Inst.* 1.2.6.

33. Ibid. 1.11.8–9.

34. Ibid. 1.11.9–11, 16.

35. Plutarch *Mor.* 178C–D.

36. Quintilian *Inst.* 1.11.17.

37. Ps. Plutarch *De educ.* 11.

38. Vegetius *Mil.* 2.14, 1.9–10.

39. Vergil *Aen.* 9.603–6.

40. John Hinderbach (1418–1486), humanist and churchman, later (after 1465) Bishop of Trent, is most famous for his role in persecuting Jews after the alleged ritual murder of Simon of Trent.

41. Ps. Plutarch *De educ.* 13.

42. Ibid. 11; Plato *Resp.* 537B.

43. Jerome *Ep.* 125 (*PL* XXII 1075).

44. Jerome *Ad Iovinian.* 2.10 (*PL* XXIII 299C).

45. Juvenal 11.11–15.

46. Basil of Caesarea *Ad adolesc.* 9.25.

47. Jerome *Ad Iovinian.* 2.10 (*PL* XXIII 300A).

48. Suetonius *Aug.* 74 (where the point is referred to Augustus); and John of Salisbury *Policraticus* 8.7 (*PL* CIC 734C).

49. Suetonius *Aug.* 76; John of Salisbury *Policraticus* 8.7 (*PL CIC* 735A).

50. John of Salisbury *Policraticus* 8.7 (*PL CIC* 735A); Suetonius *Calig.* 58.

51. *Convivia*, from *cum* and *vivo*, "living together." Cf. Cicero *Sen.* 13.45.

52. Aulus Gellius *N. A.* 19.2.7.

53. Ibid. 19.2.3–7.

54. Macrobius *Sat.* 2.8.15.

55. Plutarch *Cato Mai.* 8.1.

56. Jerome *Ep.* 52 (*PL XXII* 536); a paraphrase of Lev. 10:9 (Vulg.).

57. Jerome *Ad Iovinian.* 2.11 (*PL XXIII* 301A).

58. John of Salisbury *Policraticus* 8.8 (*PL CIC* 379A); Valerius Maximus 6.3.9.

59. Plutarch *Mor.* 173E.

60. Aulus Gellius *N. A.* 15.2.5–7; cf. Plato *Leg.*, Bks. I-II.

61. Aulus Gellius *N. A.* 15.2.8.

62. Cicero *Fin.* 5.30.92.

63. John of Salisbury *Policraticus* 8.8 (*PL CIC* 737C–D).

64. Basil of Caesarea *Ad'adolesc.* 9.12–14.

65. Plutarch *Mor.* 786A.

66. Basil of Caesarea *Ad adolesc.* 9.26.

67. Ibid. 9.3, 5.

68. Ps. Plutarch *De educ.* 8; Plato *Grg.* 470E; Cicero *Tusc.* 5.12.35.

69. Basil of Caesarea *Ad adolesc.* 5.9; Plutarch *Mor.* 78C.

70. Ps. Plutarch *De educ.* 11.

71. An old proverb: Theognis 159–60; Vergil *Georg.* 1.461; Macrobius *Sat.* 2.8.2; Aulus Gellius *N. A.* 13.11. Also the title of one of Varro's lost *Menippean Satires*.

72. Cicero *Tusc.* 3.14.29.

73. Plutarch *Mor.* 176D.

74. Aristotle *Pol.* 1287a-b.

75. Sirach 10:3 (Vulg.).

76. Vegetius *Mil.* 1 (pref.)

77. I Kings 3.9 (Vulg.)

78. Plutarch *Mor.* 178F.

79. Cicero *Tusc.* 1.26.64.

80. Plutarch *Mor.* 189D.

81. Quintilian *Inst.* 1.1.15–16.

82. Ibid. 1.1.4–6.

83. Cicero *Tusc.* 1.30.72; cf. Plato *Apol.* 41A.

84. Basil of Caesarea *Ad adolesc.* 2.1–7.

85. Math. 6:33 (Vulg.)

86. Valerius Maximus 1.1.9.

87. John of Salisbury *Policraticus* 4.3 (*PL* CIC 516B-C).

88. Clement of Alexandria *Epist. ad Corin.* 57.1, 63.1.

89. Ps. Plutarch *De educ.* 6.

90. Vergil *Georg.* 2.272.

91. Ps. Plutarch *De educ.* 17.

92. Basil of Caesarea, *Ad adolesc.* 9.26–27.

93. Aulus Gellius *N. A.* 17.17.2

94. Cicero *Off.* 1.25.85; Plato *Resp.* 420B.

95. Homer *Od.* 1.356–59.

96. Cicero *Off.* 1.22.77.

97. Cicero *Inv. rhet.* 1.4–5.

98. Ps. Plutarch *De educ.* 9, 14.

99. Horace *Epist.* 1.18.71.

100. Ps. Plutarch *De educ.* 9.

101. Aulus Gellius *N. A.* 1.9.3–4, 1.15.11.

102. Lit. 'breast', considered by the ancients to be the seat of the spirit.

103. Ibid. 1.15.1–5; Homer *Il.* 3.221, 4.350.

104. Aulus Gellius *N. A.* 1.15.16.

105. Ibid. 1.15.13; said of M. Lollius Palicanus in Sallust *Hist.* 4.43.

106. Ps. Plutarch *De educ.* 9.

107. Quintilian *Inst.* 1.11.1, 4, 6–8.

108. Ibid. 1.11.37.

109. Ibid. 11.3.54.

110. Ibid. 1.1.22.

111. Ibid. 1.3.7.

112. Ps. Plutarch *De educ.* 14.

113. I Cor. 15:33 (Vulg.).

114. Jerome *Ep.* 70 (PL XXII 665); idem *Comm. in Epist. ad Galat.* (PL XXVI 389); idem *Comm. in Epist. ad Eph.* (PL XXVI 525); idem *Comm. in Epist. ad Titum* (PL XXVI 571).

115. Basil of Caesarea *Ad adolesc.* 4.2–3; Homer *Od.* 12.165–200 (where Odysseus actually places wax in the ears of his comrades but listens to the sirens' song himself).

116. Ps. Plutarch *De educ.* 14.

117. Ibid.

118. Juvenal 8.140–41.

119. Ps. Plutarch *De educ.* 9.

120. Quintilian *Inst.* 1.3.1.

121. Ibid. 1.1.36.

122. Ps. Plutarch *De educ.* 13 (9F); Hesiod *Op.* 360–61.

123. Quintilian *Inst.* 1.7.34.

124. Ibid. 1.6.19.

125. Psalms 2.10 (Vulg.). The royal prophet is King David.

126. Quintilian *Inst.* 1.4.2–3.

127. Ibid. 1.5.3.

128. Ibid. 1.5.55–58, 60.

129. Vergil *Ecl.* 3.50.

130. Ibid. 3.44, 46.

131. Ibid. 3.78.

132. Vergil *Aen.* 3.354.

133. Quintilian *Inst.* 1.5.61.

134. Ibid. 1.5.68, 71.

135. Ibid. 8.6.5–7.

136. Ibid. 8.6.7.

137. Ibid. 8.6.14.

138. Augustine *Serm.* 220 (PL XXXIX 2152).

139. Quintilian *Inst.* 8.6.15.

140. Ibid. 1.5.72, 8.3.34.

141. Horace *Ars P.* 70–73.

142. Horace *Carm.* 4.15.20.

143. Ibid. 2.17.24–25.

144. Servius *in Aen.* 6.661.

145. Horace *Ars P.* 58–62.

146. Quintilian *Inst.* 8.3.34–35.

147. Ibid. 1.5.3–4.

148. Ibid. 1.4.12–13.

149. Ibid. 1.6.10–11. *Pepigi* is now considered the perfect form of *pango*, not *pago*.

150. Ibid. 1.6.10–11.

151. Ibid. 1.5.8–12.

152. Vergil *Ecl.* 1.32.

153. Vergil *Aen.* 8.274.

154. Juvenal 4.28–29.

155. Quintilian *Inst.* 1.5.15, 18.

156. Vergil *Aen.* 1.2.

157. Quintilian *Inst.* 1.5.35–36. A proper response would be "Me quidem."

158. Ibid. 1.5.46.

159. The correct interrogative would be "An hic aut ille fuerit?"

160. Ibid. 1.5.50.

161. Exod. 20.15 (Vulg.).

162. I.e., *nex* is not attested in good authors in the nominative case nor *mortes* in the plural with the verb *immineo*.

163. Because *manes* is not attested in the singular.

164. Quintilian *Inst.* 1.5.52–54.

165. Ibid. 1.6.1.

166. Ibid. 1.6.4–10. The word is regularly declined *ferveo, ferves, fervet*.

167. Vergil *Aen.* 4.409. Modern texts give *litora fervere late*.

168. Quintilian *Inst.* 1.6.12.

169. Ibid. 1.6.28–29.

170. Ibid. 1.6.32, 34.

171. Gen. 1:10 (Vulg.)

172. Quintilian *Inst.* 1.6.34–36.

173. Ibid. 1.6.37–38.

174. Ibid. 1.6.32.

175. Ibid. 1.6.30.

176. Ibid. 1.6.39–40.

177. Aulus Gellius *N. A.* 1.10; Macrobius *Sat.* 1.5.1–2.

178. Macrobius *Sat.* 1.4.19.

179. The quotations, respectively, are from Vergil *Aen.* 12.208, *Ecl.* 3.69, and *Ecl.* 1.15; the citatations come via the passage of Quintilian that Aeneas Silvius is following here.

180. Quintilian *Inst.* 1.6.2.

181. Ibid. 1.6.41–42.

182. Macrobius *Sat.* 1.4.18.

183. Quintilian *Inst.* 1.6.42–43.

184. Cicero *Tusc.* 3.9.20.

185. Ibid.

186. Macrobius *Sat.* 1.15.17.

187. Aulus Gellius *N. A.*, 10.24.5, 10.24.8. Pomponius is Pomponius Lucius, a writer of farces who flourished in the time of Sulla.

188. Ibid. 1.4.22–23.

189. Quintilian *Inst.* 1.6.43–44.

190. Ibid. 1.6.45.

191. Ibid. 1.4.4.

192. Ibid. 1.8.5.

193. Augustine *De civ. Dei* 1.3.

194. Cicero *Sen.* 1.3, 8.26, 11.38; Jerome *Ep.* 52 (*PL* XXII 529).

195. Cp. Cicero *Off.* 1.65: *principem . . . se esse mavult quam videri*

196. Cicero *Tusc.* 1.2.3.

197. Ibid. 2.11.27; Plato *Resp.* 398A.

198. Boethius *Cons.* 1.1.

199. Jerome *Ep.* 22 (*PL* XXII 416)

200. I.e., the medieval commentators and glossators on the corpus of Roman law.

201. Cicero *Tusc.* 1.2.3, 2.11.27–12.28.

202. Cicero *De or.* 1.9.38.

203. Aulus Gellius *N. A.* 19.11.

204. Tit. 1:12 (Vulg.); cf. Diels-Kranz, *Fragmente der Vorsokratiker* II (Berlin, 1907), 493–94.

205. I Cor. 15:33 (Vulg.).

206. Jerome *Ep. 70* (*PL* XXII 665–66).

207. Basil of Caesarea *Ad adolesc.* 4.1.

208. Jerome *Ep. 70* (*PL* XXII 665).

209. Basil of Caesarea *Ad adolesc.*, 4.9–5.2.

210. Horace *Epist.* 1.2.69–70.

211. Macrobius *Sat.* 5.1.

212. Apollonius of Rhodes

213. Lucius Annaeus Seneca, the tragedian and philosopher, was actually the son of the much less famous Lucius Annaeus Seneca, a writer on declamation.

214. The tragedy referred to here is the *Progne* of Gregorio Correr (1409–1464), a student of Vittorino da Feltre; on the *Progne* (based on the story in *Metamorphoses* 6) see Joseph R. Berrigan, "Latin Tragedy of the Quattrocento," *Humanistica Lovaniensia*, 12 (1973), 1–9.

215. Cicero *De or.* 2.9.36.

216. Pliny the Younger *Ep. 3.5*.

217. Alfonso I of Aragon, King of Naples (1443–58), called "the Magnanimous" for his generous patronage of arts and letters.

218. Vergil *Georg.* 4.6.

219. I.e., penmanship and spelling.

220. Aeneas Silvius refers broadly to humanistic script (ancient) and Gothic script (modern); the latter is the ancestor of German *Fraktur* and was the more widely used script in fifteenth century Germany.

221. Ibid. 2.156.

222. Priscian *Inst.* 1.45 (Keil, II 35). This reference, along with those to *Gram. Lat.* that follow, may have come via an intermediary source.

223. Albericus *Orth.* (Keil, VII, 295f.).

224. Quintilian *Inst.* 1.7.7–8.

225. Priscian *Inst.* 1.43 (Keil, II 34).

226. Vergil *Ecl.* 3.96.

227. Ovid *Amores* 1.15.1.

228. Statius *Theb.* 10.936.

229. Ibid. 4.603.

230. Ibid. 2.479.

231. Quintilian *Inst.* 1.4.11.

232. Priscian *Inst.* 1.39 (Keil, II 30–31).

233. Pomponius Porphyrio *Com.* (Keil, V, 231).

234. Priscian *Inst.* 1.44 (Keil, II 34).

235. Velius Longus *De orth.* (Keil, VII, 65).

236. Ibid. (Keil, VII, 66); Albericus *Orth.* (Keil, VII, 310–11).

237. Quintilian *Inst.* 1.7.5.

238. Ibid. 1.7.28.

239. Vittorino da Feltre (1370–1446), a famous humanist schoolmaster who taught at the court of the Gonzaga in Mantua.

240. Ibid. 1.7.6; Marius Victorinus *Ars gram.* (Keil, VI, 13). Gasparino Barzizza (d. 1431) was a professor of rhetoric at Pavia and Padua and the author of a treatise on orthography which made a significant contribution to the humanist effort to replace medieval spelling with that of classical Latin.

241. Quintilian *Inst.* 1.7.10.

242. Phoca, *De aspir.* (Keil, VIII 356).

243. Servius *in Georg.* 2.233; Cicero *Orat.* 160.

244. Priscian *Inst.* 1.24–26 (Keil, II 18–21).

245. Aeneas Silvius is probably referring to the translation of George Trebizond, made in 1443–45 for Alfonso of Aragon, King of Naples.

246. Possibly to be identified with the *Rhetorica* of the early German humanist Petrus Luder.

247. Aeneas Silvius here summarizes the five parts of rhetoric from pseudo-Cicero's *Rhetorica ad Herennium*.

248. Cicero *Fat.* 1.1.

249. Cicero *Off.* 1.6.19. A standard argument for the active life as against the contemplative.

250. Quintilian *Inst.* 2.20.3.

251. John of Salisbury, *Policraticus* 1.7 (*PL* CIC 404B-C); Suetonius *Ner.* 20–22.

252. Plutarch *Mor.* 67F.

253. Quintilian *Inst.* 1.10.19.

254. Ibid. 1.10.13.

255. Ibid. 1.10.22.

256. Ibid. 1.10.14.

257. Ibid. 1.10.27; Aulus Gellius *N. A.* 1.11.10.

258. I Sam. 16:14–23 (Vulg.); John of Salisbury *Policraticus* 1.6 (*PL* CIC 401B).

259. Quintilian *Inst.* 1.10.15.

260. Ibid. 1.10.10; Vergil *Aen.* 1.740–46.

261. Quintilian *Inst.* 9.4.12.

262. John of Salisbury *Policraticus* 1.6 (*PL* CIC 401A); Gen. 4.21 (Vulg.).

263. Quintilian *Inst.* 1.10.34.

264. Ibid. 1.10.48. For the story, see Plutarch *Marc.* 14–19. Archimedes was said to have used his knowledge of geometry and mechanics to invent various machines used against the Romans at the siege of Syracuse.

265. Quintilian *Inst.* 1.10.39–43.

266. Ibid. 1.10.47–48.

267. Ibid. 1.4.4.

268. Ibid. 1.12.1–7.

269. Ibid. 12.1.19.

270. John of Salisbury *Policraticus* 7.5 (*PL* CIC 644A).

271. Quintilian *Inst.* 12.2.10; John of Salisbury *Policraticus* 7.5 (*PL* CIC 644A). "Rational philosophy", i.e., metaphysics.

272. Ps. Plutarch *De educ.* 10.

A PROGRAM OF TEACHING AND LEARNING

1. I.e., from lineage; ancient Roman patricians treasured the death-masks of their ancestors in household shrines to remind them of their family virtues and traditions.

2. Juvenal 8.

3. Cicero *De or.* 2.44.186.

4. Ovid *Fast.* 1.216.

5. Ps. Plutarch *De educ.* 7; Cicero *Tusc.* 5.4.10–11. Sea travel was considered much more dangerous than land travel in premodern times.

6. An allusion to Juvenal 3.164, a famous line.

7. Quintilian *Inst.* 2.9.1.

8. Plutarch *Alex.* 8.3.

9. Sallust *Cat.* 51.3

10. Cicero *Flac.* 20.47.

11. Horace *Epist.* 1.2.70–71.

12. Quintilian *Inst.* 2.3.2–3.

13. Ps. Plutarch *De educ.* 12; Quintilian *Inst.* 1.3.13–14.

14. Ibid. 1.2.21–22.

15. Ibid. 1.2.13–15.

16. Ovid *Pont.* 4.2.35.

17. The reference here is to the famous *Regulae*, composed when Guarino was teaching in Venice and derived ultimately from Priscian but simplified and brought in line with classical sources. It was widely used through the fifteenth century and printed in 1484.

18. I.e., they will not know how to attach endings to their stems.

19. In this system verbs are divided into five classes: active, passive, neuter, common, and deponent.

20. The six classes are *activum simplex* (with only the object in the accusative case), *activum possessivum* (with this accusative plus a genitive), *activum acquisitivum* (with accusative and dative), *activum transitivum* (with two accusatives), *activum effectivum* (accusative and ablative), and *activum separativum* (accusative and ablative with *a*).

21. An example would be *aro terram*, to be distinguished from *doceo*, which governs two accusatives.

22. I.e., except words whose stem ends in a vowel.

23. Augustine *De mus.* 3.7–4 (*PL* XXXII 1124–48).

24. The reference is to the *Doctrinale* of Alexander of Villedieu, written in 1199.

25. Juvenal 8.126.

26. Vergil *Aen.* 6.239–42.

27. Ovid *Met.* 7.418–19.

28. Ibid. 8.151.

29. Ovid *Fasti* 4.63; cf. Plato *Cra.* 406C.

30. Vergil *Aen.* 7.324.

31. Ibid. 4.383–84.

32. Ibid. 10.199.

33. Quintilian *Inst.* 1.1.12.

34. Cicero *Acad.* 2.2.5; idem *Sen.* 8.26. Cato famously learned Greek when he was an old man.

35. Horace *Ars P.* 268–69, 323–24.

36. Quintilian *Inst.* 1.1.12.

37. The references are to Chrysoloras's *Erotemata*, the elements of Greek grammar presented in question-and-answer form, and to the abridgement made by Guarino when he was teaching in Venice; Guarino's abridgement was printed in Venice in 1484.

38. I.e., irregular verbs.

39. Cicero *Orat.* 8.25.

40. Horace *Ars P.* 309.

41. Cicero *Nat. D.* 2.24.63–25.64.

42. I.e., remaining chaste and avoiding remarriage.

43. Jerome *Ep.* 282 (*PL* XXII 554); Terence *Eun.* 732.

44. Augustine *De civ. D.* 1.3.

45. Quintilian *Inst.* 10.1.90.

46. I.e., the deliberative genus of rhetoric: the part of rhetoric concerned with making speeches in deliberative assemblies.

47. Cicero *Amic.* 89; cf. Cicero *Att.* 7.3.10.

48. Quintilian *Inst.* 10.1.99.

49. Macrobius *Sat.* 2.1.10.

50. I.e., the *De sphaera* of Sacrobosco, a popular Latin manual of astronomy, geography and chorography, digested into Italian by Leonardo Dati in the mid-fifteenth century.

51. The elder Guarino dedicated his Latin translation of Strabo's *Geography* to Pope Nicholas V (1446–1455).

52. Florence, Biblioteca Nazionale, MS Naz. II.I.67 (*olim* Magl. VI.25) contains the observations of Guarino on the *Ad Herennium*, recorded by Battista.

53. In Italian Renaissance schools it was customary to have the older students help in teaching the younger ones.

54. I.e., without ritual cleansing or due preparation (a phrase from Aulus Gellius)

55. The elder Guarino lectured formally on Augustine's *City of God*; the inaugural oration to his course of lectures survives and is published in K. Müllner, *Rede und Briefe italienischer Humanisten* (Vienna, 1899; rpr. Munich, 1970).

56. Pliny the Younger *Ep.* 3.5.10.

57. Ibid. 3.5.17.

58. Plutarch *Mor.* 130B.

59. Pliny the Younger, *Ep.* 9.36.3.

60. Plutarch *De rect. rat.* 8 (*Mor.* 42B)

61. Cicero *De or.* 2.3.10.

62. The *clausula* is the rhythmic ending of a sentence; the correct prose-rhythm to be used in *clausulae* was a major topic of medieval rhetorical handbooks.

63. I.e., literally.

64. Xenophon *Cyr.* 1.4.3; Plutarch *Cat. Min.* 1.5.

65. Hesiod *Op.* 361–62; ps. Plutarch, *De educ.* 13 (*Mor.* 9F); the latter work is the one translated by the elder Guarino, not Hesiod.

66. Cicero *Arch.* 16.

67. Pliny the Younger *Ep.* 1.9.6.

68. Ibid. 1.9.8.

69. Ibid. 3.5.16.

70. Ibid. 3.5.12.

71. Cicero *Fin.* 3.2.7.

72. Cicero *Tusc.* 3.28.69.

73. Lit. 'by right of teaching'; Battista means that since he stands to his student Maffeo *in loco parentis* (see cap. 4, above), his own father Guarino can be considered Maffeo's grandfather.

Bibliography

꩜

Black, Robert. *Humanism and Education in Medieval and Renaissance Italy*. Cambridge: Cambridge University Press, 2001. An important empirical study of classroom practice.

Bushnell, Rebecca W. *A Culture of Teaching: Early Modern Humanism in Theory and Practice*. Ithaca and London: Cornell University Press, 1996. An interesting extension of some of the issues raised by Italian humanist education into the English environment.

Garin, Eugenio, ed. *Il pensiero pedagogico dello Umanesimo*. Florence: Giuntine / Sansoni, 1958. A generous selection of primary source material on humanist education with Italian translations and notes.

Giannetto, Nella, ed. *Vittorino da Feltre e la sua scuola: Umanesimo, pedagogia, arti*. Civiltà veneziana, saggi, 31. Florence: Olschki, 1981. A useful collection of essays on an important educator.

Grafton, Anthony, and Lisa Jardine. *From Humanism to the Humanities: Education and the Liberal Arts in Fifteenth- and Sixteenth-Century Europe*. Cambridge, Mass.: Harvard University Press, 1986. A revisionist study of humanist educational theory and practice.

Grendler, Paul. *Schooling in Renaissance Italy: Literacy and Learning, 1300–1600*. Baltimore: The Johns Hopkins University Press, 1989. Comprehensive survey of Italian Renaissance education.

The Humanism of Leonardo Bruni: Selected Texts. Translations and Introductions by Gordon Griffiths, James Hankins, and David Thompson. Medieval and Renaissance Texts and Studies, 46. Binghamton, N.Y.: MRTS, 1987. An indispensable introduction to the life and works of Bruni.

McManamon, John. *Pierpaolo Vergerio the Elder: The Humanist as Orator*. Medieval and Renaissance Texts and Studies, 163. Binghamton, N.Y.: MRTS, 1996. Excellent survey of the life and works of Vergerio.

Sabbadini, Remigio. *La scuola e gli studi di Guarino Guarini Veronese*. Catania: F. Galati, 1896. Classic study of Battista Guarino's father and his teaching methods.

Voigt, G. *Enea Silvio de' Piccolomini als Papst Pius der Zweite.* 3 vols. Berlin: G. Reimer, 1856–63. The standard study of Piccolomini, still not superseded.

Woodward, William H. *Studies in Education during the Age of the Renaissance 1450–1600.* Cambridge: Cambridge University Press, 1906; reprint New York: Columbia University, 1967. An older but still helpful collection of essays.

Index

References are to paragraph numbers; capital letters refer to the treatises by Vergerio (V), Bruni (B), Piccolomini (P), and Guarino (G); "n" refers to the notes.

Accius, Lucius, B20, P57
Achilles, P9
Admetus, B26
Aemilius Lepidus, Marcus, V59
Aemilius Paullus, Lucius, P94
Aeneas, B27
Albericus, P78n223, P83n236
Albert, King of Hungary and Bohemia, P3
Alcestis, B26
Alexander of Villedieu, G15n24
Alexander the Great, V10, V49, V54, V55, P8, P9, P12, P26, P73, P90, G4
Alfonso I of Aragon, King of Naples, P75n217, P89n245
Alighieri, Dante, V47n108
Ambrose, B7, P31, P72
Apollo, B26
Apollonius of Rhodes, P69n212
Archimedes, P93n264
Architas of Tarentum, P4
Ariston, G33
Aristophanes, P28
Aristotle, V2n3, V8n15, V11n22, 23, 24, 25, V12nn26, 28, 29, V14nn33, 34, 35, 37, 38,

V15nn39, 40, 41, V27n68, V41nn92, 93, V42nn94, 97, V43n99, V48nn109, 111, V49, V62nn139, 140, V70nn151, 152, B11n12, B16, B20, B26, B29, P9, P18, P26n74, P89, G28
Arrian (Lucius Flavius Arrianus), P73
Aspasia, B1
Atilius, G37
Augustine, B2, B7, B15, B20, B29, P45n138, P61n193, P72, G14n23, G24n44, G3n55
Augustus, Emperor, V54, V68, P17, P40, P47, P91
Aurelius Victor, Sextus, V32n80, V33n82
Aurelius Victor, Sextus, pseudo, V31n72, V32nn79, 80, V61n138
Aurunci, tribe, P55

Barzizza, Gasparino, P84n240
Basil of Caesarea, B7, P16n46, P21n64, P22n66, P23n67, P25n69, P29n84, P32n92, P38n115, P66n207, P68n209
Bathsheba, B27

Bible, V13n32, V19n50, V21n54,
    B27nn30, 31, 32, 33, 34, 35,
    P2nn2, 3, P4n10, P5nn12, 13,
    P19n56, P26nn75, 77, P30n85,
    P38n113, P40n125, P46, P50n161,
    P54n171, P65nn204, 205, P67,
    P73, P91n258, P92n262
Boethius, Anicius Manlius
    Severinus, B20, P4n8, P62n198,
    P64, P97
Bracciolini, Poggio, P72
Brescia, V59
Bruni, Leonardo, P72, V39n89

Caelius Rufus, Marcus, P54
Caesar, Julius, V10, V54, V71,
    B18, P4, P17, P40, P54, P55
Caligula, Emperor, P17
Carthage, V59
Cato. See Porcius Cato, Marcus
Catullus, P70
Chrysippus, P10, P12, P28
Chrysoloras, Manuel, V39n89,
    G18n37, G35
Chrysostom, John, B7
Cicero, V1n2, V4n8, V6nn10, 13,
    V10n20, V15n40, V16n42,
    V18n48, V21nn52, 53,
    V26nn64, 65, V27n68,
    V29nn69, 71, V31n73, V32n77,
    V34nn84, 85, V37n87, V39n88,
    V42n94, V46n106, V52n118,
    V53n119, V55n124, V56n126,
    V58n128, V60nn135, 137,
    V72n155, V73n156, V74n157,
    B1n2, B2n6, B8, B9n9, B11nn11,
    12, 13, B14nn14, 15, B17n17, B20,

B29n37, P7n17, P20n62,
    P25nn68, 72, P27n79, P29n83,
    P33n94, P34nn96, 97, P40,
    P43, P45, P46, P57nn184, 185,
    P61n194, P62nn195, 196, 197,
    P63n201, P64n202, P65, P72,
    P73n215, P86n243, P89,
    P90nn248, 249, P97, G1n3,
    G3n5, G4n10, G17n34, G21n39,
    G23n41, G24, G25n47, G27,
    G28, G33n61, G34, G37n66,
    G39nn71, 72
Cicero, pseudo-, P89n247
Claudian (Claudius Claudianus),
    P69
Claudius, Emperor, V31
Claudius Marcellus, Marcus, P4,
    P93
Clement of Alexandria, P31n88
Constantine, Emperor, P31
Cornelia, second daughter of
    Scipio "Africanus," B1, P28
Cornelius Scipio "Africanus" (the
    Elder), Publius, V10, V34,
    V59, V69, B1, P4, P45, P63
Correr, Gregorio, P71n214
Coruncanius, Tiberius, P55
Crates, P8n18
Crete, V56
Curius Dentatus, Manius, P55
Curtius Rufus, Quintus, B18, P73
Cyprian, B7, P65
Cyrus the Great, King of Persia,
    P19, G35

Daphne, B26
Dati, Leonardo, G26n50

David, B27, P40n125, P91
Decembrio, Uberto, V39n89
Demetrianus, P65
Demetrius I of Macedonia, "Besieger of Cities," P25, P27
Demetrius of Phalerum, B1n3, P27
Democritus, B29, P37
Demosthenes, B14, P23, P34, P36, P89
Dido, B27
Diogenes the Cynic, P23
Diogenes Laertius, V9n16, B24n24, P8
Dion of Syracuse, P4, P94
Dionysius II, tyrant of Syracuse, P25, P94
Domitian, Emperor, V32, V33, V34

Ennius, Quintus, B20, P53, P56, P62, P63
Epaminondas of Thebes, P4
Epicharmus, P35
Epicurus, B16
Epimenides, P65
Eratosthenes, P28
Eugene IV, Pope, P75
Euripides, B20, B26n27, P25, P38
Eustathius, P18

Fabius Maximus Verrucosus "Cunctator," Quintus, V10, P4
Fabius Pictor, Quintus, P53
Fabricius Luscinus, Gaius, P55
Favorinus, P55
Firmianus, Lucius Caecilius, P65

Francesco da Carrara, brother of Ubertino, of Padua, V68
Francesco da Carrara (the Elder), ruler of Padua, V1n1, V3n7
Frederick III, Holy Roman Emperor, P17, P75
Frontinus. See Iulius Frontinus, Sextus
Furia, G23

Gambara, Maffeo, G1, G39n73
Gellius, Aulus, P18nn52, 53, P20nn6, 64, P25n71, P33n93, P35nn101, 103, 104, 105, P55n177, P57nn187, 188, P64n202, P91n257, G29n54, G31
George of Trebizond, P89n245
Giacomo da Carrara, brother of Ubertino, of Padua, V68
Gorgias, P25
Governolo, battle of, B25n25
Gracchus. See Sempronius Gracchus, Tiberius
Gregory of Nazianzus, B7
Gregory of Nyssa, P72
Guarino da Verona, P72, G8n17, G18n37, G26n51, G27n52, G31n55, G36n65, G39n73

Hannibal, V59
Hesiod, B20, P28, P39n122, G19, G36n65
Hinderbach, Johann, P14n40
Homer, V55n125, V70n150, B20, B21nn18, 19, B22, B26nn26, 29, P33n95, P35n103, P38n115, P61, P65, G19

Horace, V12n27, V66n143,
V69n147, P34n99, P46n141,
P47nn142, 143, 145, P68n210,
P70, G4n11, G17n35, G21n39
Hortensius Hortalus, Quintus,
P23, P49
Hyginus, G26

Ioppas, P91
Isocrates, G33
Iulius Frontinus, Sextus, V66n144

Jacopino, ruler of Padua, V3n6
Jacopo II, ruler of Padua, V3n6,
V31
Jerome, V13n32, V21n54, B2, B7,
B20, B29, P15nn43, 44,
P17n47, P19nn56, 57, P38n114,
P61n194, P62n199, P65n206,
P67n208, P72, G23n43
Jesus, B22, P29
John of Salisbury, P2n1, P4nn7, 9,
P17nn48, 49, 50, P19n58,
P20n63, P31n87, P91nn251, 258,
P92n262, P96nn270, 271
Justin (Marcus Iunian[i]us
Iustinus), P73, G22
Juvenal, P3nn4, 5, 6, P10nn27, 30,
P16n45, P38n118, P49n154,
P70, G1n2, G3n6, G16n25, G25

Lactantius (Lucius Caelius
Firmianus), V31n73, B2, B7,
B20, B22n23, B29, P72
Ladislas, King, P1, P2, P25
Laelius, Gaius, V69, G25
Larcius Licinus, G31

Leonidas, P8, P9
Lepidus. *See* Aemilius Lepidus,
Marcus
Licinius Egnatius Gallienus,
Publius, Emperor, V31
Livy, B8, B18, P73
Lot, daughter of, B27
Lucan, P69, G24
Lucullus, P21
Luder, Petrus, P89n246
Lycurgus, V56, V69, P91

Macrobius, Ambrosius
Theodosius, P18n54, P25n71,
P55nn177, 178, P56n182,
P57n186, P64, P69n211,
G25n49, G31
Malatesta, Battista, B1
Malatesta, Carlo, B25n25
Malatesta, Galeazzo, B1
Marcellus. *See* Claudius
Marcellus, Marcus
Marius, Gaius, V63, P61
Marsilietto, ruler of Padua, V3n6
Martial, P70
Martianus Minneus Felix Capella,
G26
Megara, P25
Menander, V13n32, P38, P65
Messala, P47, P56
Milan, B25n25
Mincio (river), B25n25
Minos, V56
Mithridates, King, P33
Modena, V54
Moses, P92
Mucius Scaevola, Quintus, V69

Nero, Emperor, V31n76, P8, P17, P49, P91

Nicaea, Council of, P31

Nicholas V, Pope, P75, G26n51

Nicias, P94

Nobilior, Marcus, P62, P63

Novello, Francesco, ruler of Padua, V1n1, V3n6, V58n127

Ovid, B1n3, B26n28, P69, P71n214, P80n227, G3n4, G6n16, G16nn27, 28, 29, G24

Pacuvius, Marcus, B20

Palicanus, Marcus Lollius, P35n105

Parthia, V66

Paul the Apostle, V13, P38, P65

Paulus, Lucius. See Aemilius Paullus, Lucius

Peleus, P9

Penelope, B26

Pericles, P4, P34, P94

Persius, P70, G25

Peter, Saint, P31

Philip, King of Macedon, V49, P9, P12, P26, P91, G4

Philostratus, Lucius Flavus, V71n153

Phocas, P86n242

Phoenix, P9

Pindar, B20

Plato, V1n2, V6nn12, 13, V21n55, V31n73, B1n4, B20, B21, B24n24, B26, B29, P4n8, P12, P14n42, P20n60, P21, P25n68,

P27, P29n83, P33n94, P62n197, P63, P64, P94, P96, G16n29, G28

Plautus, P71, G25

Pliny the Elder (Gaius Plinius Secundus), G31, G38

Pliny the Younger (Gaius Plinius Caecilius Secundus), P73n216, P97, G31nn56, 57, G33n59, G37nn66, 67, G38nn69, 70

Plutarch, V1n2, V9n16, V18n47, V34n85, V54n125, V60nn135, 136, V63n141, V69n148, V70nn150, 152, P4, P8, P10, P12n35, P18n55, P19n59, P21n65, P25nn69, 73, P26n78, P27n80, P38nnI12, 116, 117, 119, P91n252, P93n264, G4n8, G33nn58, 60, G35n64

Plutarch, pseudo-, V2nn3, 4, V11n21, V13nn30, 31, V17n44, V25n60, V27n66, V32n78, V48n112, V54n121, P4n9, P6n15, P9n22, P10nn25, 28, P11n31, P13n37, P14nn41, 42, P25nn68, 70, P32nn89, 91, P34n98, P35nn100, 106, P39n122, P97n272, G3n5, G5n13, G36n65

Pompey, Gnaeus, P21

Pompey, Sextus, P90

Pomponius, Lucius, P57n187

Pomponius Mela, G26

Pomponius Porphyrio, P80n233

Porcius Cato, Marcus, "the Censor," V26, V52, P4, P18, P56, P61, G17n34, G35

Porcius Cato, Marcus, "Uticensis,"
    V34, G38
Priscian, B4, P59, P78n222,
    P79n225, P80n232, P81,
    P86n244, G8n17, G15
Procne, P71n214
Propertius, P70
Ptolemy (Claudius Ptolemaeus),
    G26
Pythagoras, B20, P21, P96
Pythagoreans, V70, B24n24, P35,
    P92, G31

Quintilian, V5n9, V6n10, V7n14,
    V10n20, V22n56, V24n58,
    V26nn62, 65, V27n67, V35n86,
    V40n91, V42nn95, 96, 97, 98,
    V44n101, V45n102, V47nn107,
    108, V48n110, V49nn113, 115,
    V51n116, V52n117, V53nn119,
    120, V70n149, B1n2, B6n7,
    B9n9, B14n14, P6n14, P8nn18,
    19, P9nn20, 21, 23, 24, P10nn26,
    28, 29, P11n32, P12nn33, 34, 36,
    P28nn81, 82, P36nn107, 108,
    109, P37nn110, 111, P39nn120,
    121, P41nn126, 127, P42nn128,
    133, P44n134, P45nn135, 136,
    137, 139, P46n140, P47nn146,
    147, P48nn148, 149, 150,
    P49nn150, 155, P50nn157, 158,
    159, 164, P52n165, P53nn166,
    168, P54nn169, 170, 172, 173,
    174, 175, P55n176, P56nn179,
    180, 181, P57n183, P58nn189,
    190, P60n191, P61n192,
    P78n224, P80n231, P84nn237,

238, 240, P85n241, P89,
    P90n250, P91nn253, 254, 255,
    256, 257, 259, 260, P92n261,
    P93nn263, 264, 265, P94nn266,
    267, P95n268, P96nn269, 271,
    G4nn7, 12, G5n13, G6nn14, 15,
    G17n33, G18n36, G24n44,
    G25n48, G27, G29

Rimini, B25n25
Rusticus, P15
Rutilius Rufus, Publius, V63

Sacrobosco, G26n50
Sallust, V3n7, V10n17, B8, B18,
    P35n105, P73, P97, G4n9
Samson, B27
Sappho, B1, P70
Sardanapullus, P16
Saul, P91
Scaevola. See Mucius Scaevola,
    Quintus
Scipio Africanus. See Cornelius
    Scipio "Africanus" (the Elder),
    Publius
Sempronius Gracchus, Tiberius,
    P91
Seneca the Younger (Lucius
    Annaeus Seneca [2]), V2nn3,
    5, V3n7, V10n19, V16n43,
    V17nn44, 45, V18nn46, 49,
    V23n57, V26n63, V27nn66, 67,
    V31n75, V33n81, V40n90,
    V46n105, V48n111, V51n116,
    V54n123, V59n129, V60n135,
    B28, B29, P8, P71n213, P97,
    G25

Servius, B4, P47n144, P86n243

Sibyl, Cumaean, B22

Sicani tribe, P55

Socrates, V9, V26, V43, B1, B21, P4, P8, P12, P18, P25, P29, P91, G3

Sodom, inhabitants of, B27

Solinus (Gaius Iulius Solinus), G26

Solomon, B27, P26

Sparta, V18, V49, V56, V60, V69, P19, P91

Statius, B28, P69, P70nn228, 229, 230, G24

Stilpon of Megara, P25

Strabo, G26n51

Suetonius, V10n18, V3nn74, 75, 76, V32n79, V33n82, V54n122, V71n154, P17nn48, 49, 50, P73, P91n251

Sulpicius Apollinaris, Gaius, P90, P94

Syracuse, P93n264

Tacitus, B18

Taddea d'Este, wife of Francesco Novello, ruler of Padua, V1n1

Terence, V14n36, P47, P71, G23n43, G25

Tereus, P71

Thales, P96

Themistocles, V1, P91

Theocritus, G19

Theodosius, Emperor, V61, P31

Theognis, P25n71

Theophrastus, B29, G38

Theseus, P25

Tibullus, P70

Ticino (river), V59

Timotheus, V49, P9, G4

Titus, Emperor, V32

Trajan, Emperor, P8

Traversari, Ambrogio, B7n8, P72

Trieste, P1

Tubal, P92

Twelve Tables, P48, P55

Ubertino da Carrara, ruler of Padua, V1n1, V3n6, V30, V59nn132, 133, V74

Ulysses, B26

Uriah, B27

Valerius Maximus, V20n51, V26nn64, 65, V31n73, V34n85, V59nn130, 131, V63n142, V69n142, V70n150, P19n58, P30n86, P73, G22

Varro, Marcus Terentius, B29, P25n71, P53, P54

Vegetius Renatius, Flavius, V67n144, P13n38, P26n76

Velius Longus, P82n235, P83n236

Venus, B26

Vergil, V25n61, V29n70, V49n114, B8, B1on10, B21n20, B22nn20, 21, B25n25, B26n29, B27n36, B28, P13n39, P25n71, P32n90, P42nn129, 130, 131, 132, P49nn152, 153, 156, P53n167, P56n179, P61, P69, P70, P75n218, P77n221, P80n226, P91n260, G15, G16n26, G17nn30, 31, 32, G19, G24, G25

Vespasian, Emperor, V32
Victorinus, Marius, P84n240
Vitellius, Aulus, Emperor, P17
Vittorino da Feltre, P71n214,
    P84n239
Vulcan, B26

Wendel, Kaspar, P5n11

Xenophon, V6n11, V54n125,
    G35n64

Zeno, B16

Publication of this volume has been made possible by

The Myron and Sheila Gilmore Publication Fund at I Tatti
The Robert Lehman Endowment Fund
The Jean-François Malle Scholarly Programs and Publications Fund
The Andrew W. Mellon Scholarly Publications Fund
The Craig and Barbara Smyth Fund
for Scholarly Programs and Publications
The Lila Wallace–Reader's Digest Endowment Fund
The Malcolm Wiener Fund for Scholarly Programs and Publications